Rent2Rent

Landlords, Agents, Tenants & The Legal Skills You Need To Consider

Taiwo Orishayomi

authorHOUSE®

AuthorHouse™ UK Ltd.
1663 Liberty Drive
Bloomington, IN 47403 USA
www.authorhouse.co.uk
Phone: 0800.197.4150

Published by AuthorHouse   09/10/2013

ISBN: 978-1-4918-7731-9 (sc)
ISBN: 978-1-4918-7732-6 (hc)
ISBN: 978-1-4918-7740-1 (e)

Book Two

When I wrote the first book, I did not think I would create a second volume. But when I realised that so many people had jumped on the bandwagon, I thought it would be prudent to write a second volume that covered the legal aspect of property management.

People management is a skill, and property management can be learned.

I hope that, with the help of the contents of this book, you will understand the code of conduct that Rent2Rent requires. There are laws and regulations in place; let us all apply them and abide by them.

In this second volume, you will read about some of my experiences with landlords, agents, and (most frequently) tenants. The last chapter addresses different acts of Parliament and regulations that have been passed over the past fifty years and relate to property law in England and Wales.

This book is aimed at those who already practice Rent2Rent strategy. It also caters to those who wish to try out this strategy one day. Finally, this book serves as a guide for landlords, especially those who manage their own portfolio.

As standard practice dictates, please consult your solicitor on all legal matters.

*"If you are passionate about your work,
you will never work a day in your life"*

quote from unknown

This book was not created for property experts, gurus, property investor 'Facebookers,' or forum junkies. Rather, this book was created for those who want to make it in the property business in today's tough economic climate.

In short, this book was designed for people like me.

I dedicate this book to my mother, Folashade Olawumi. You have always been my inspiration and my source of energy. You are my shero.

I also dedicate this book to all my students who have entrusted me with enthusiasm. I hope I have not failed. Likewise, I hope I never fail you. Your inquisitive minds have pushed me to sharpen my knowledge in order to pass my wisdom on to you. I hope I have provided you with the scaffolding upon which you can build your unique businesses.

INTRODUCTION

This is a guide to landlord and tenant law. It is the set of rules all Rent2Rent managers must adhere to. We are tenants *and* acting managers. Our acute knowledge of the law is key to our success in managing tenant and landlord expectations.

Usually, a Rent2Rent property will be classified as a house in multiple occupation (HMO). Please contact your council for a licence to rent out your property as an HMO in England or Wales. A house in multiple occupancy is a property rented out to at least three people who are not from the same household but share facilities such as bathrooms and the kitchen. It is sometimes called a house share.

You must have a licence for your HMO if the following conditions are met:

- The house is rented to five or more people who form more than one household
- The house is three or more storeys high

Even if your property is smaller and rented to fewer people, you may still need a licence (depending on the area). Check with your council.

Restrictions

A licence is valid for a maximum of five years. You must renew your licence before it expires. If you run more than one HMO, you need a separate licence for each home.

Conditions

You must make sure the following conditions are met:

- The house is suitable for the number of occupants (including its size and number of facilities)
- The manager of the house—you or an agent—is considered to be 'fit and proper' (i.e., the person should not have a criminal background or a record of a breach of landlord laws or the code of practice

The landlord or agent must also do the following things:

- Send the council an updated gas safety certificate every year
- Install and maintain smoke alarms
- Provide safety certificates for all electrical appliances when requested

The council may add other conditions to your licence (e.g., improving the quality of your facilities). They will instruct you how to proceed. And if you disagree with any conditions the council sets, you can appeal to a residential property tribunal.

How to apply

Contact the council to request an HMO licence information packet. You should apply for the licence yourself, but if you use a managing agent, he or she can apply for you. You will be charged a fee, which is set by the council.

Fines and penalties

You can be fined up to £20,000 for renting out an unlicensed HMO.

Your rights and responsibilities

In all privately rented property, you will have certain rights and responsibilities.

Your rights

As a tenant, you have the right to the following things:

- To live in a property that is safe and in a good state of repair
- To have your deposit returned when the tenancy ends (and in some circumstances have it protected)
- To challenge excessively high charges
- To know who your landlord is
- To live in the property undisturbed
- To see an energy performance certificate for the property
- To be protected from unfair eviction and unfair rent
- To have a written agreement if you have a fixed-term tenancy that lasts more than three years

If you have a tenancy agreement, it should be fair and comply with the law. If you don't know who your landlord is, ask (in writing) the person or company you pay rent to. If he or she doesn't give you that information within twenty-one days, he or she may be fined.

Your responsibilities

You must give your landlord access to the property to inspect it or carry out repairs. Your landlord has to give you at least twenty-four hours' notice and visit at a reasonable time of day, unless it is an emergency and he or she needs immediate access.

You must do the following things:

- Take good care of the property (e.g., turn off the water at the mains if you are away when it is cold outside)

- Pay the agreed rent, even if repairs are needed or you are in dispute with your landlord
- Pay other charges as agreed upon with the landlord (e.g., council tax or utility bills)
- Repair or pay for any damage you (or those for whom you are responsible) cause
- Sublet a property only if the tenancy agreement or your landlord allows it

If you do not fulfil your responsibilities, your landlord has the right to take legal action to evict you.

Your landlord's safety responsibilities

Your landlord must keep the property you are renting safe and free from health hazards.

Gas safety

Your landlord must do the following things:

- Make sure the supplied gas equipment is safely installed and maintained by a Gas Safe registered engineer
- Have a registered engineer carry out a gas safety inspection on each appliance and/or flue annually
- Give you a copy of the gas safety check record before you move in or within twenty-eight days of the check

Electrical safety

Your landlord must make sure of the following:

- That the electrical system (e.g., sockets and light fittings) is safe
- That all appliances supplied (e.g., cookers and kettles) are safe

Fire safety

Your landlord must do the following:

- Follow fire safety regulations (e.g., ensuring that you have access to escape routes at all times)
- Make sure furniture and other supplied furnishings are fire safe
- Provide fire alarms and extinguishers (depending on the size of the property)

Repairs

What your landlord must do

Your landlord is always responsible for repairs to the following areas:

- The property's structure and exterior
- Basins, sinks, baths, and other sanitary fittings (including pipes and drains)
- Heating and hot water
- Gas appliances, pipes, flues, and ventilation regions
- Electrical wiring
- Any space he or she damaged when attempting to repair something

Your landlord is usually responsible for repairing common areas such as staircases in blocks of flats. This information should be in your tenancy agreement.

Your responsibilities

You should only carry out repairs if the tenancy agreement says you can. You cannot be forced to do repairs that are your landlord's responsibility. If you damage another tenant's flat, however, you are responsible for paying for the repairs. You are also responsible for paying to put right any damage caused by your licencees, family and friends.

If your property needs repairs

Contact your landlord if you think repairs are needed. Contact him or her straight away for faults that could lead to health problems, such as faulty electrical wiring. You should continue to pay your rent while waiting for repairs to be completed, but your landlord should tell you when you can expect everything to be finished.

If repairs are not done

If your request has gone unanswered, ask your local council's environmental health department for help. Your council can make the landlord take action if the property contains health and safety hazards.

Rent increases

Your tenancy agreement should include how and when the rent will be reviewed.

When your landlord can increase rent

Your landlord cannot normally increase the rent more than once per year without your agreement. With a fixed-term tenancy (running for a set period), your landlord can only increase the rent if you agree; if you do not agree, the rent can only be increased when the fixed-term ends.

General rules around rent increases

For any tenancy, the following rules apply:

- Your landlord must get your permission if he or she wants to increase the rent by more than previously agreed
- The rent increase must be fair and realistic (i.e., in line with average local rents)

How your landlord must propose a rent increase

If the tenancy agreement lays down a procedure for increasing rent, your landlord cannot deviate from that procedure. Otherwise, your landlord can take one of the following actions:

- Renew your tenancy agreement at the end of the fixed term, but with an increased rent
- Agree to a rent increase with you and produce a written record of the agreement that you both sign
- Use a *landlord's notice proposing a new rent* form, which increases the rent after the fixed term has ended

Your landlord must give you a minimum of one month's notice unless you have a yearly tenancy. In the case of the latter situation, he or she must give you six months' notice. If you think the rent increase is unfair, you can apply to a rent assessment committee who will decide the rent amount.

Rent arrears

If you get behind with your rent, your landlord may evict you. That eviction may result in the loss of the house. Shelter has advice and information if you are in rent arrears or having difficulty paying rent. It recommends talking to your landlord and trying to come to an agreement with him or her.

Always read any letters from your landlord because they may contain information about actions your landlord is going to take.

Going to court over rent arrears

If you cannot reach an agreement with your landlord, he or she can ask a court to evict you.

Deposit protection

Usually, your landlord must place your deposit in one of three government-approved tenancy deposit protection schemes. The schemes help make sure you get your deposit back if you meet the terms of your tenancy agreement.

In England and Wales, if you rent your home on an assured shorthold tenancy that began after 6 April 2007, your landlord must place your deposit in one of the following tenancy deposit protection (TDP) schemes:

- Deposit Protection Service
- MyDeposits
- Tenancy Deposit Scheme

There are two new schemes available as of 1 April 2013:

- Capita Tenancy Deposit Protection
- Deposit Protection Service Insured

These government-backed schemes ensure that you will get your deposit back if you meet the following criteria:

- Adhere to the terms of your tenancy agreement
- Avoid damaging the property
- Pay your rent and bills

Your landlord or letting agent must put your deposit in the scheme within thirty days of getting it.

At the end of your tenancy

If you and your landlord agree upon how much of your deposit will be given back, that money must be returned to you within ten days of the tenancy ending. If you are in a dispute with your landlord, your deposit is protected in the TDP until the issue is sorted.

Holding deposits

Your landlord does not have to protect a holding deposit (money you pay to hold a property before an agreement is signed). However, once you become a tenant, the holding deposit becomes a deposit that must be protected.

Deposits made by a third party

Your landlord must use a TDP scheme even if your deposit is paid by someone else, such as a rent deposit scheme or your parents.

A practical guide to evicting a troublesome tenant

Sections 8 and 21: Notice to Quit

Section 8 notice to quit: This notice is used to end a tenancy before the expiry of the fixed term of an assured shorthold tenancy agreement. Section 8 notices usually require a court application in order to be enforced. The tenant has no obligation to vacate until a court order for possession (and possibly rent arrears) is made.

Section 21 notice to quit (assured shorthold or periodic tenancy): This notice is used to end a tenancy after the expiry date of a fixed term of an assured shorthold tenancy agreement, but it can be served at any time during a tenancy.

- Providing the section 21 notice is valid, the tenant must vacate. No grounds for eviction are required. A county court application for possession will only be necessary if the tenant does not vacate.
- Section 21 notices to quit do not deal with rent arrears. If the tenant vacates on receipt of the notice, recovery of rent arrears may prove difficult.

LANDLORDS

nen I decided to find landlords willing to work with me, I first asked myself two questions: *Why would any landlord give me his house so I could make money? Why wouldn't he manage his own portfolio and make the most of it?*

I then took myself back to when I first had the idea to multi-let my own home because I was struggling financially. If you have read my first book, you will know that, after spending all my money on property courses with a 'guru' who did not even practice what he was coaching, I nearly lost everything. I had just a few days to find tenants who could move into my house; otherwise, I wouldn't be able to pay my mortgage. I found three Italian men who were looking for a landlord who could accommodate all three of them in a house. The rest is history.

When I decided to seek people like myself, I first contacted letting agents. I approached quite a lot of them, but I was saying the wrong things. Consequently, none of them gave me any attention, let alone showed me a house.

I then decided to post a simple advert on Gumtree. I explained who I was and what I was looking for. What follows is an approximation of what I wrote; it was an impulsive advert, so I did not save it anywhere:

I am a landlord who works with local employers to find accommodations for their foreign employees. I am looking for landlords with empty houses in Fishponds and around the city centre for a long-term contract. My company will guarantee the rent and cover all maintenance costs. A weekly cleaner will ensure that your house is maintained well.

Please call me for further information.

I was surprised when I received a call from a landlord who happened to have a very large portfolio of 200 properties. I later discovered that about sixty were located in Bristol, some of which were empty. He had a management company, but the volume of work was getting out of hand. He just wanted the houses to be taken care off. The money was not the main issue, as I later discovered. Basically, he did not want empty properties. As I now know, empty property means squatters, vandalism, and a lot of pain.

One of the main problems for many landlords with large portfolio is finding the right partners. I found that many professional landlords opened their own agencies in order to manage their portfolio, but they did so without knowing how to drive their agencies and staff. Simple tasks were left undone frequently, and before they knew it, there was no order to the business.

The landlord who contacted me was glad to find me. Likewise, I was glad to find him. I was more than lucky to find him, actually, because I took seven properties off his hands within a few weeks. We still work together to this day.

My experience with my second landlord was not as good, however. I found her through an agent. She was looking for a tenant, but she did not want the agent to manage the house for her. That didn't bother me. We signed a contract for twelve months, and at the end of the tenancy agreement, she asked me whether I would like to renew my contract. I agreed. Within the first two months after signing the renewal contract, I encountered problems with the house. There were some repairs that needed to be done, but she refused to do them. For example, a tile had shifted from one side of the roof, which allowed rainwater to enter one of the rooms. I alerted her, but she didn't do anything about it. And then the bathtub split down the middle. It was a very old tub, and it needed to be changed. I informed her of the problem, but she said it was my fault that it split and that I had to replace it myself. And then the entrance door started to jam. Again, I drew her attention to the issue. She responded by sending someone to apply superglue to it. I understood that she was going through some financial difficulties and wanted to sell the house, but unfortunately, she decided to make things very uncomfortable for me.

Because I was tied down to a contract with her, leaving the property would mean losing my deposit. Therefore, I discussed the matter with my city council who advised me to contact the environmental department. After I consulted with the department, they sent someone to look at the house and ordered the landlord to make some repairs to the house. Reluctantly, she made the repairs. At that stage, however, I just wanted to be out of the contract. Thus, I sent a letter to inform her that I would leave after six months. She agreed. On my last day, the inventory clerk arrived along with her and with her son. She brought numerous things to the clerk's attention, but the clerk repeatedly told her that the repairs she was referencing were part of the normal wear and tear. When she realised that she could not get her way, she decided to pull her wild card: she noted that I was illegally subletting rooms. At that time, I did not have my section 3 form, so she got away with murder and never returned my deposit.

After that, I drafted a form that all my landlords must sign if they wish to work with me. The form states what I do and authorises my actions. Subletting is not illegal as long as you have the consent of the landlord.

The lesson I learned from my experience was that I could never trust anyone. I learned that I always had to have my agreements in writing. In short: property means greed! People will take advantage of you whenever they can. I am including this fact in the book to aid novices and those eager to be financially free. I cannot stress enough the necessity to have some form of knowledge before parting with your money. I hope that this book will give you enough nuggets to move forward one step at a time.

When I say *property means greed,* I mean that some of the people you meet may want to use you, especially when you have ideas and share them naively (as I did). If you do not have the correct paperwork in place, landlords or agents could take advantage of you if they change their minds. Use this book as a quick guide or as a stepping stone towards further learning.

Now back to my experiences with landlords. I found my third landlord through an agent as well. I never met him; instead, we communicated via email. I know that he manages his own portfolio and uses agents to find long-term tenants.

We signed an initial term of three years. As of this writing, we have been working together for two years. He has never increased the rent, and whenever a repair job needs to be done, I do it and send him an invoice. His company settles with me at the end of the month. I even handle all the gas safety checks for him. This type of landlord commands my ultimate respect. He knows how to keep a good tenant happy. Above all, he knows how to avoid screwing up a good relationship—unlike my fourth landlord, with whom I signed a two-year contract. When she bought her house five years prior the market was not in good shape. She rented the house to a Chinese guy who used to pay her £900, cash in hand, which was £200 above market rate. She discovered a year later that her entire house had been transformed into a cannabis farm. By that time, the whole house was destroyed. She had to spend over £5,000 to get the house in good condition again. And then she rented it to a group of students who never paid on time. She had to go there weekly to collect her rent.

Can you imagine an elderly woman doing that? Needless to say, she got fed up of the whole thing by the end. She gave the house to an agency with the hope of finding a long-term professional let. I came along and showed my willingness to take the house; we then signed for two years.

During that time, I always paid my rent three days before the due date. I always kept her in the loop in terms of the state of the house. I did not meet her until two months before the end of my tenancy agreement. When we met at the house and I showed her around, she was over the moon about the state of her property. I told her that I was also a landlady and that all my Rent2Rent houses were treated just like hers. And then she dropped a bomb: she told me that the agency who found me contacted her and told her she could get £250 more per month for the house due to the current market. I told her that I had just signed a contract on another house just a few yards away from hers and that the price was just £50 above what I was currently paying her.

I also reminded her of the maintenance cost that I never passed onto her and many other advantages she would lose if she increased her rent above the norm. To cut a long story short, she decided to go with the advice of the agent. And I decided not to convince her otherwise; she was quite set on what she was told by the agent. Consequently, I had to move my tenants into another property.

One thing about Rent2Rent is that the landlords get fat and comfortable, forgetting what it's like to have parasite as tenants. Experience has taught me many valuable things. For one, I have managed to secure my investments—be it my time or money—through some legal documents that can be found at the end of this book. One of these legal documents is the *option to renew clause,* which can be included in your contract. This means that you can secure a property for a long term if you secure the right to renew once the initial term has been fulfilled. The landlord cannot say no, and you can choose not to exercise that right if you do not wish to. Yes, you read right. No joke!

I have been asked by many people why I don't buy my Rent2Rent houses. The reason is simple: none of the landlords want to sell. When they are being paid on a regular basis and are not bothered by streams of repairs, why bother?

Earlier, I was talking about greed. One of my landlords embodies that vice. The landlord was recommended to me; someone who knew her said she was struggling to rent out her four-bedroom house. I visited it and found out that the house was good enough and in the right location, so I signed for a year with the possibility of buying it later.

I knew she wanted to sell when she was struggling. Remember when I said that a landlord is not likely to sell when there is no pain? My mistake was taking the house as Rent2Rent; I should have suggested buying it from the start. Mind you, those were my early days and I did not know much. The truth is, I was not ready to buy it. I thought it would be wise to rent for a while in order to learn all the ins and outs of the property. And then, if it was good enough, I could make my move to buy it.

After a year, she approached me for a renewal. I asked whether she still wanted to sell and she replied in the negative. Therefore, I decided to sign for another year. A short while later, she was approached by a buyer who had just bought a house next door. The offer must have been too good to miss. Thus, she sought a way to end my contract and pin the blame on me.

She came to the house one Sunday and spoke with my tenants. She told them that I was subletting without her consent. She told them not to pay rent and asked whether they wanted to sign a new contract with her and pay less. She knew that that arrangement would net her more money. Greed came into play, turning the whole situation into a huge mess. My tenants forgot all the services I provided (i.e., broadband, a weekly cleaner, most utilities, and appliance maintenance), and the landlord forgot the peace of mind my presence gave her. Consequently, they all came together to kick me out.

I agreed to leave provided my deposit was returned and the tenants signed an agreement indicating that they were putting an end to their contract with me at their own risk. I also got the landlord to agree that I would not be held responsible for anything that happened once my contract was terminated. In the end, she got her house and kept the tenants.

What the tenants did not know was that a house was being built in their garden and the application was being processed with the city council. The landlord did not know that I was in the process of evicting two of the three guys for always submitting their rent late. Even though I reminded them constantly, I still didn't get the money on time. I believe they had just lost their jobs. The landlord lived in Wales; how on earth was she going to chase the rent payments? Also, if it were not for my presence in the house, the guys would smoke the curtain and wallpaper. I knew that, the moment I was out of the picture, they would destroy the house in a matter of weeks with their smoking and other deleterious actions. Greedy people and fools do make a good marriage. I just sat back and watched the house crumble to dust.

The last thing I heard regarding that house was that the council rejected the plans to build a new house in the garden and the landlord who offered to buy her flat changed his mind. Therefore, she was stuck with the same tenants in the house. I believe there was a *to let* or *for sale* sign in front of the house. Who do you think had the last laugh?

Most of my landlords are looking for a short financial break and just holding until the market recovers so they can sell. My next landlord was introduced to me by one of my agents. He was going to move into the new house with his fiancée, but the relationship fell apart. Thus, he decided to live with his parents until he came back to his senses. He needed to rent it out quickly, so I got it for £200 below the market rate. I signed for a year.

The landlord was a great guy. He was managing his house and lived close by, so whenever there was something wrong, he came straight away to discuss a way to resolve the issue. He trusted my expertise, and most importantly, he trusted my tradesmen. They never overcharge and always do the best work.

At the end of the year, he decided to move back into the house. I was rather disappointed because I had just signed new tenants to the house. I asked whether he wanted more money, and to my surprise, he declined. That was the first for the industry. Anyway, we arranged to move out once I sorted out new places to live for my current tenants.

He moved back in within weeks, but after just four weeks, he called to ask whether I wanted to rent three out of the five rooms. He said he wanted me to have them and was recommending me to some friends of his who had properties. I initially agreed to help him, but I later decided to help with advice instead of getting so involved. The guy had great respect for me, so I did not want that relationship to change. I advised him how to market the rooms and for what prices. Similarly, I gave him tips about what to include in the rent and what furniture to buy.

I even helped him draft some contracts that would protect him as a landlord living with tenants. By doing things that way, he would get to keep all his money and pick who lived with him. He is one of the landlords with whom I have become friends.

Most of my landlords are people who live abroad. They bought their houses many years ago—perhaps thirty years or more prior—so they are not concerned about money. All they want is enough money to finance their lifestyle in Spain, Australia, China, or Africa. Many of the landlords have PAs or family members who oversee some matters for them, but most importantly, I manage the properties for them. They always use agents to find tenants, but I have manoeuvred my way into gaining their trust and dealing directly with them. Many of these landlords never used to increase their rent (or if they did, it was only by a small amount). They have since learned that it is better to increase the rent moderately and keep a good tenant than to inflate the rent and lose a good tenant.

It is easier to find bad tenants than good ones. I always tell my landlords that they will never find a better tenant than me. I know it sounds odd, but it's true: I am the best asset they will have on their property. I will always give a house back upgraded, *never* downgraded. This is why it is important for me to sign a long-term contract because, when they see the upgrade, they will want to put it on the market as a result of the value gained.

Eviction—my experience

The eviction process is not very interesting. My eviction experience is limited to just three episodes, thankfully. The people I evicted were all Local Housing Allowance (LHA) tenants. The council made it easy to get them into my houses, but made it very hard to evict them. When I say *hard*, I mean they told them that I could not get them out until they had spent at least six months in the house. They basically told them not to worry about paying what they owed because there was nothing I could do to get them out. I do not believe the council gave them that message word for word, but it was certainly implied. The council kept paying their share of the rent, but the tenants did not keep up with theirs.

I approached the council as a way to limit my voids to a strict minimum. I will not say that all LHA tenants are like the ones I got. I know many landlords and letting agents who mainly deal with that market. One needs to have the right knowledge before sailing into any kind of market. Unfortunately for me, I did not have that knowledge at the time. Today, however, I do, and I have a couple of LHA tenants on my books who are great assets to my business.

In order to keep my voids to a strict minimum, I contacted the council and told them that I had a few rooms available. They came to have a look at the house. I had already dealt with all the security concerns (e.g., the gas certificate, Portable Appliance Test (PAT) on all portable appliances, and energy Performance Certificate (EPC), so it was no hassle. The agreement was that the council would pay two-thirds of the rent and the tenant would pay the rest. The council respected their part of the agreement, but the tenants did not. They had money to throw parties and get drunk by eleven o'clock in the morning, but they did not have money to pay £40-£80 top-up.

As soon as I realised the rent was not being submitted, I notified the council. At first, they were very helpful. They called the tenants and advised them to make amends. I was quite unfortunate to have professional parasites as tenants. I believe that good values are not contingent upon one's economic status; rather, it varies by personality. I have no respect for anyone who thinks that others should be responsible for them. Good or bad moral values will always show who we are, regardless of our wealth.

I read somewhere that If one does not give when poor, one will never give when wealthy. Here is my twist: 'if one does not take responsibility for his or her actions when poor, he or she will never take responsibility for himself or herself when wealthy.' You can add your own twist to the sentence; the possibilities are endless.

After a few months of going back and forth with the council, I finally decided to get them out of my houses. The council pulled a complete reversal on me and said I could not get rid of them until their contract was up. The person who had been helping me up until then became largely unavailable. I called another department of the council to ask for legal advice for private landlords and was referred to the private tenancy team. The person I needed to speak to came to work only on Tuesdays and Thursdays. Thus, I had to be a bit patient.

I was the first person to call him one Tuesday. He was pretty helpful. He took my e-mail address and sent me the section 21 and accelerated repossession of property forms. I sent the section 21 form to the tenants and filled out the other form, which I sent to the court.

The court sent me an acknowledgement letter and a copy of my form to the tenants. The court gave them a certain number of days to either pay the outstanding rent or face eviction. None of them took any action. They knew what they were doing; they had seen it before. They knew they could gain more weeks by not responding.

When the grace period cooled off, the court sent them a move out date. At that point, two months had passed since the court action. The court said they would send bailiffs if the tenants did not move by that date. Luckily, they all moved out, curiously leaving half of their belongings behind.

The court ordered them to pay my fees, but they knew very well that I would never retrieve my costs let alone the arrears. I think that the system should make it easier for landlords to kick out anyone abusing the system. I was very lucky that my cases were quite trouble free, but the process was still too long. The council paid only a month's rent in damage. I asked them about the rest, but they told me they could do nothing more.

I shared that experience with a fellow investor who has a large portfolio of LHA tenants. He explained to me that I should always ask the tenant for a private guarantor who owns a property. He told me that that was the only sure way to receive what was due.

Tip: when dealing with an LHA tenant, always secure a guarantor who lives, works, and owns a property in England or Wales.

AGENTS AND BASIC LAW

The Association of Residential Letting Agents

The Association of Residential Lettings Agents (ARLA) is the only professional and regulatory body for letting agents and letting agencies in the United Kingdom.

By using a Licensed ARLA agent, you are guaranteed the following:

- **That the agency is covered by the Client Money Protection (CMP) scheme**
  - o The ARLA has the ability to make discretionary grants (up to preset limits) if you suffer financial loss due to the bankruptcy or dishonesty of the member and/or his or her firm
- **That the agency has professional indemnity insurance**
  - o This ensures you are financially covered for successful claims relating to members' negligence, bad advice, or mishandling of data
- **That you are consulting with a qualified and trained agent who can give you professional, up-to-date advice and guidance**
  - o All members are required to carry out at least a minimum level of Continuous Professional Development (CPD) each year, though many do much more
- **That you are dealing with an agent who voluntarily follows the code of practice and rules of conduct laid down by his or her professional body**
  - o If an agent does not follow the code, he or she can be fined or expelled from the ARLA. The disciplinary process includes everything from cautions and warnings to more severe penalties of up to £5,000 for each rule breached. You can be sure that the highest standards are upheld by the members.

As a Rent2Rent manager, it is important to observe the same rules as a qualified agent—especially the ones related to the health and safety of your tenants and those who work with us.

The Health and Safety at Work Act (HASAWA) is the main piece of legislation covering health and safety at work. It is supplemented by other regulations and codes of practice. It is designed to ensure the health and safety of everyone: employers, employees, and clients.

For example, if you use your car to carry potential tenants to viewings, make sure that you have business insurance to cover you. By doing an Internet search, you should be able to get a few quotes for good professional indemnity coverage.

When you are doing viewings, always arrive a few minutes early to ensure that the property or room is safe. Check slippery surfaces, particularly during the winter or rainy season. Ensure that the house is tidy and devoid of hazards. Always mentally carry out a risk assessment before bringing in a potential tenant.

Here are some basic things to check for before showing a potential tenant a house:

- Trailing wires or cables
- Loose carpet or flooring
- Stairs and steep inclines
- Sharp objects left lying around

The HASAWA concerns should not take more than a few minutes to assess and redress.

Who would have thought that all my civil studies classes I completed in my teens would become useful twenty-odd years later. Yes, I am referring to the law that governs all of us. I had to learn about these laws specifically because I was raised in France, but the basic knowledge is more or less the same.

As a Rent2Rent manager, the knowledge of the law will come in handy more often than one thinks. In fact, my bad tenants often wonder about the way I handle things, so I need to keep them quiet. The only way to do that is to know more than they think they know. Many of these regulations came in handy when I carried out my first eviction.

I am going to take you back to some basics. Most of this is common sense but not common practice. I hope that, by explaining the source of these laws, they will become common practice.

The Law

The law is a mixture of legal and moral rules that govern the way in which we treat one another and the way the state treats us. The law in England and Wales can be divided into two parts:

- Private law
- Public law

Private law is the relationship between either individuals or individuals and corporate bodies.

For example:

- Law of contract (between landlord and tenant)
- Law of tort (between an agent and a landlord)

Public law outlines the relationship between the government and the local authorities (and between separate local authorities) and between individuals and corporate bodies.

Let's look at criminal and civil law. Criminal law concerns the activities that are detrimental to society as a whole. These activities are punishable by the state. In lettings, a criminal offence is breaching the Protection from Eviction Act 1977. Civil law concerns interactions between individuals and organisations that are not criminal. Any contract law will be dealt with under the umbrella of civil law.

The law of England and Wales has not been set down in an official code, unlike many other European countries. Whenever a legal problem arises, one has to look at several sources. In fact, there are six different sources of law:

- Custom law, also known as common law, is based on traditions
- Judicial precedents refer to past rulings by judges
- Books of authority
- Law commission, which is a permanent body established under the Law Commission Act 1965 to keep the law under review. It consists of a chairman and four lawyers of high standing. It is independent of the government, the law of society, and bar council. It can make proposals for change or create new laws)
- Legislation, otherwise known as statute law, is now Parliament's dominant form of law making
- European Union

Decisions made in a higher court are binding in lower courts. The highest court is the European court. Since joining the Union in 1972, many England and Wales laws have been influenced by European policies. For instance, certain health and safety laws and human rights laws are now observed as they are in other European countries.

The hierarchy of authority is as follows: European Court, Supreme Court, Court of Appeal, High Court, Chancery Division—Family Division and Crown Court, County Court—tribunals and magistrates. In lettings, we will be dealing mostly with the last court, the County Court.

Rent2Rent managers work with the public. As a result, we have to be fully aware of all the changes to laws and new regulations put in place by the Parliament. All power to make laws has been given to the Parliament, and the courts must apply them.

Estate agents are governed by a number of laws (unlike letting agents, who have deal with fewer government laws). Letting agents are mostly governed by common law. The common law is interested in protecting the landlord. It is silent about any duties owed to the tenant. Please remember this: the first duty of an agent is to protect his or her client, the landlord. Legally speaking, as a Rent2Rent manager, you are a tenant, not a client. At best, you might be considered a good contact for the agent.

Contract

During my fortnightly support webinars, my students often ask me about all the aspects of a contract. They want to know whether the contract is between the agent and the landlord or between the tenants and the landlord. They also want to know how negotiable a contract is. In short, there are many questions.

To start, for a contract to be a contract, it must have three essential elements:

- An offer
- An acceptance of an offer
- A payment/consideration

Any price issued by the landlord or agent is negotiable. This is called an *invitation to treat*. If you want the property badly, though, you can't waste time negotiating.

A contract can be ended in four ways:

- Agreement
- Performance (the contract is fulfilled)
- Breach
- Frustration (something occurs that is no one's fault; e.g., death)

I have ended a contract in agreement only twice. Otherwise, all my contracts have been fulfilled. I understand that, in some cases, a house situation might be unacceptable or the landlord might be unreasonable in terms of repairs. Remember: if you breach the contract without sufficient proof, the landlord could request damages and force you to pay remedies. Remedies are designed to put the injured party in the same position as if the contract had been fulfilled. This is one of the reasons I prefer to deal with agents instead of landlords directly.

Data Protection

Data protection is a human rights issue. The Data Protection Act 1998 enlarged the Data Protection Act 1984 to include not only paper-based data, but also electronic data. The Data protection Act 1998 allows you to collect information that is relevant to your job and renting rooms. The information collected must not be shared with a third party without the consent of the tenants. Further, any organisation processing data must be registered with the Information Commissioner's office (www. ico.gov.uk). The cost is roughly £35 per annum.

If you suspect any illegal activity you must report it to the SOCA (Serious Organised Crime Agency). If you suspect any terrorist activities, you must report it to the police under the Anti-Terrorism Crime and Security Act 2001.

In my opinion, it is essential to start your Rent2Rent business with an agent. They can handle all landlord/agent legal matters, and they tend to get the bulk of the houses from landlords who do not want to manage their portfolio. I have met several property investors who invest for the fun of it or to generate capital. They are not interested in tenant management whatsoever. All they want is to get enough to cover any expenses until they decide to sell. Most of these landlords will approach letting agents without reservation.

Eighty per cent of my Rent2Rent portfolio is run directly through letting agents. It is therefore not advisable to neglect working closely with them. I know it can be hard to find the right ally, though. Many agents will be suspicious because they do not know you or trust you. But the main reason for their caution stems from their interest in meeting their landlords' and clients' needs.

Many of my students feel more comfortable working with private landlords; I felt the same way at the beginning. My beginner's luck did not last long, but my first few properties were through a private landlord. I am quite aware that it was just a matter of luck that I found him at the right time.

I found the first letting agent who agreed to work with me on Gumtree. I searched the site and found some interesting letting agents' adverts. I contacted a few, but only one agreed to do viewings with me. I met the representative of the agency in Bristol, and she showed me a few houses. We became friends, and I took several houses from her. She later became my reference for recruiting other agents. After working with that agent for about a year, the agent was sold to another agency. That resulted in three of my contracts not being renewed. It was fine, though, because I had five others that were renewed. I still have them today.

My second agent was a bit more difficult to work with. The agent needed proof of my company's track record. Unfortunately, at that stage, my company was in its first year of trading and I had not submitted a company account. The agent wanted two years' worth of accounts, which I could not provide. The agent then requested a guarantor, two references, and my bank statements. Thankfully, I had been working for four months with a private landlord and another agent. Plus, I had my sister, and she agreed to stand up as my guarantor. I also had a healthy bank statement to show them.

I became very close with the senior letting agent of that agent. I invited her for a drink one evening to better explain my plans. After a few glasses of bubbly, her favourite drink, we became best friends. Indeed, she became my first property finder.

My first property with that agent was a four-bedroom, ex-student accommodation that the landlord had managed for fifteen years. He wanted to get out of the student market because he was obliged to renovate every year when the students went on holiday. We agreed on a twelve-month deal, which we later renewed for two more years because he was convinced that I was reliable.

Within two months, my agent called me for another house just a few minutes away from the first house. It was another four-bedroom house. It was slightly more expensive, but there was still room for a healthy profit. I took it right away. She called again a couple of weeks later to show me another house owned by the same landlord; she said that the landlord specifically asked for me. I am sure that she presented me well to him. The property was perfect: it was bigger with the potential for more profit. Consequently, I took it. By that time, the agent knew what I was looking for in terms of area, size, and price, so whenever she got anything relevant, she called me first. Also, whenever a suitable house was listed with other agents, she managed to keep the set of keys long enough for me to have the first viewing. I took nine houses from her in total. I made her a lot of money, too, because she got all the commission from the landlords.

My third agent was young and full of innocent blood. They were almost completely inexperienced. By that time, I was experienced enough to give them some advice. For example, they did not know what HMO was. I had to explain to them again and again which sorts of houses I was looking for. I needed either a fully licensed, HMO, ex-student accommodation or a two-storey, four-bedroom house.

After a while, I managed to get three houses from them. The turnover of staff was so great, however, that I decided to quit working with them. Ultimately, I was spending a lot of time coaching the people who never stayed long enough for us to establish a solid collaboration.

A year later, one of the properties I took from that young agent was ready for renewal. To my great surprise, the landlord was not informed of my strategy; she specifically wanted to have a family in her house, not sharers. I did not understand her reasoning, and she became very upset about the situation. In the end, I had to leave because the agent did not discuss the nature of what I was doing with the landlord. After that incident, I enlisted a solicitor to draft a *consent to underlet* contract for all my landlords. I wanted to ensure that the agents discussed what I did with the landlords before matching me with them.

I understand that it might be an added difficulty for some, but that is what I request. Rent2Rent is a business matchmaking strategy. We help people who need our help. We work with landlords who want to work with us. We offer payment security and assurance that the house will not be damaged.

ᴀ sample of the consent form:

ᴣCATION FOR CONSENT UNDER SECTION 3 OF THE LAᵢ ᴅDLORD AND TENANT ACT 1988

Date:

Address of Agent or Landlord:

Property Address:

Dear [Landlord Name] or [On Behalf of Name]:

As a relocation agent for international professionals working with well-known local organizations, I hereby request your consent to underlet to the above mentioned professionals the lease of the above premises dated [_____], effective [_____] until the end of the extension of assured shorthold tenancy agreement.

All the duties stipulated under the Tenancy Agreement remain my responsibility. I would be pleased to provide you with more information about the assignee upon request.

Sincerely,

[Your Name]

I always advise my students to modify the consent form according to their market.

Many assume that subletting a property is illegal. I asked all my agents before starting to work with them. They all told me that, as long as all parties are well aware of the deal, there is nothing illegal. I then searched the law books and found the clause that is not often used by tenants. I knew that there was nothing wrong with underletting, but finding the support in the law books was quite a challenge. Even the agents did not know about the clause.

The most important thing while working with agents is honesty and open communication. If they know what you do, it will be easier for them to match you with the right landlord. I often detect mental barriers in the minds of some students regarding work with agents. But those barriers don't have to be permanent. It took me some time to overcome my own mental obstacles. After I completed my first and second deals, my confidence grew bigger and stronger until I saw that I could train the agents to work with me. In short, I no longer need to go to them; they come to me.

I still believe that working with agents is the fastest way forward. One might get a lot of rejections. That's what happened to me in the beginning because I did not know how to approach them. Besides, I thought I was doing something wrong.

Rejection is part of the journey. If we really want it to happen, it will happen. Getting the houses is easy, but working on our minds in order to get the houses is difficult. I think that a bit of personal development is a must in any endeavour. If you can afford it, spending some money on personal development is a good investment. Otherwise, you can read or listen to personal development materials every day to build that mental strength. I have done both and continue to do both. They are now part of my daily routine.

Tip: a list of interesting books is listed in the first book (*Rent2Rent: Massive Ca$h During a Massive Crash*). Why not take a look?

WORKING
WITH
THE COUNCIL

I have been asked opinion many time in regards to working with the council. The reason I wanted to work with the council was to ensure that my rooms did not stay empty for too long. When I found out about the number of young people on the waiting list, I realised that there might be an opportunity there. Unfortunately, the first three tenants I got from the council did not impress me. I had to take all of them to court towards the end.

I know of several landlords who specialise in the LHA market and do very well. I went into that market with my eyes shut and paid the fair price for my mistakes. If you are considering going into that market, there are a few things to keep in mind. When you contact your local council, they will usually be happy to receive your call. After all, they are looking to work with private landlords; the government is not building any new homes, and the government's stock is running out. There is a fixed rate for each council.

Here is the website you will need to consult in order to learn how much you'll get from an LHA tenant: https://lha-direct.voa.gov.uk/search.aspx. Remember: even though the rent might be low, it is a sure stream of income. The tenants tend to stay longer as compared to the private market.

When you call your local private renting team, they will need assurance that your house is adequately safe. Therefore, you will be required to have all appliances PAT tested, the gas safety certificate in order, and the EPC up to date. They will also require the rooms to have locks on them. Those were the requirements they gave me when I approached them.

My first tenant was a young man, about twenty-five years old. He was a very nice chap, but he had a lot of mental issues. He constantly smoked in the house, which was against the rules, and spent his first week chopping down all the trees in the garden because he wanted to plant his potatoes. When I found out about the latter incident, there was nothing much I could do apart from telling him to ask me before making any alterations to the house. Most alarmingly, he attacked one of the girls who lived in the house because he thought she was the whistle-blower in terms of his smoking. I had to remove him from the house immediately to keep the peace. I later gave him a deadline to move out. When I spoke with his case worker, she admitted that he had been battling with anger problems. That would have been a very precious piece of information if it were given at the beginning. I was very lucky nothing serious happened during his stay at the house.

My second LHA tenant was a young girl, approximately twenty years old. She approached me directly. She was working part-time and made a very good impression. She connected me with her social worker so I could get more information about how I would be paid. Everyone was very helpful; she moved into the house within a week. Everything was fine until about three weeks later when I discovered that she was a party girl. She invited all sorts of men into the house to drink until morning, disturbing everyone else in the house. I confronted her as soon as I caught wind of the situation. She calmed down for a few weeks, but then she started up again. I told the other tenants to call me when a party was going on so I could tackle the problem. They did one night at about eleven o'clock at night. I drove to the house immediately and found a dozen guys and the girl drinking and laughing in the garden. They were not only disturbing the other tenants, but also the neighbours. I went into the garden and asked them all to leave immediately. I told them to pick up all the cans of beer on their way out and never set foot in the house again. None of them said a word. They just moved out peacefully, even apologising for the nuisance. I never saw them again.

I would not recommend that anyone try that type of confrontation. Managing people is a skill that can be learned; that is what I coach. Confidence comes with experience, and experience comes with knowledge.

The problems continued with her when she started missing her top-up payments of round £25 per month. After a few months, she decided to stop paying altogether. She waited for me to take action against her. Three months before the end of her contract, the council stopped paying her rent. At that time, I did not realise it was her payment that was stopped; I thought it was that of another LHA tenant I was evicting. When I realised my mistake, I called the council. They told me that she had full-time employment and was no longer entitled to any housing benefits. I confronted her immediately, and she told me she was not going to pay. She said she had no intention of moving out, either. I started the eviction process with her straight away. By that time, I knew the routine—she was the second person I evicted.

Because she owed two months' rent at that stage, I started a small claims court at the same time as the eviction process. When she saw how much I was going to get from her, she decided it was not worth the hassle and left my house.

I never got my money back. I did not have an address to forward the court mails to, so I learned my lesson the hard way. My precious piece of advice, then, is to ask for a guarantor who owns a house in the United Kingdom when taking on an LHA tenant.

My third LHA tenant was a young guy, also in his early to mid-twenties. He was very good looking and handsomely built. He was working as a part-time photographer at a zoo. He later got fired for being drunk on the job. He must have been bored out of his mind to do that.

He spent a lot of his time in the house getting drunk on cider. I often thought to myself, *Why would a good looking man destroy himself in such a wasteful way?*

He was unable to pay his top rent fee of £40. It piled up for six months, and I knew he would never pay. Thus, I decided to help him out of his misery by asking him to leave. I think he needed hard experiences to snap him out of his so-called depression. It took me a couple of months to get him out.

Tip: when taking on an LHA tenant, always ask for a guarantor who owns a house in the United Kingdom. In case of any trouble, the guarantor has a lot more to lose. Request any top up rent as soon as possible in writing. Always keep records of any communication.

TENANTS

The names used in this chapter have been modified to protect the guilty and the innocent.

Gemma the hooker

Gemma contacted me out of the blue one day. I could sense that she needed a room the same day. I did not want to pry, because I thought she might be running away from a nasty domestic situation. I arranged to meet her that same afternoon. She looked like she was in her mid-twenties. She was quite eager to take the room—she even had enough cash in her bag to pay me the deposit and the first months' rent. Actually, though, this situation is not terribly unusual. Indeed, many people have called me on a Sunday evening for a viewing and taken the room straight away. The only odd thing about Gemma was that she looked like a high-paid escort. I don't have any personal issues with that occupation as long it is not forced upon the woman. Ultimately, I decided to give her a chance. She paid on the spot and moved in the same day. I gave her a three-month contract. When it was time for her to pay for the second month, however, she did not return my calls. After a few days of trying to get in touch with her, I decided to pay her a visit. Her room was devoid of meaningful belongings but full of junk. There were empty bottles of alcohol, a few coke bags, and *plenty* of condoms. I decided to close the book on her at that point. I had her deposit to cover the second month, so I just put the room back on the market.

Raveen

How do I start with Raveen? He called me from abroad because he was seeking a room near his place of work. I happened to have a large double room just five minutes from his work. He viewed two of my rooms. One was a ten-minute drive to his work and the other was a five-minute walk. One was £370 and the other was £420. I had no idea he was also talking with my colleague, Riccardo. After seeing both rooms, he decided to go for the £420 one but haggled with me over the price. I told him that my final price was £420. He tried his hardest, but I still refused. He then told me he was going to view another house close to his office. I said

'Okay, call me if you want my room.' I then drove to my next viewing. At that time, Riccardo called and told me he had been speaking with Raveen who wanted the room for under £400. He told him that he would give it to him for £410. I was furious about the situation, but the damage was already done.

Curiously, Raveen refused the lower offer and called Riccardo again to negotiate the price. At that stage, I was so annoyed that I told Riccardo to tell him to piss off. Within ten minutes, Raveen called back asking whether he could visit the office to sign the paperwork. He arrived within ten minutes. He sat on my right-hand side and started to haggle over the price again. Riccardo told him that I was the decision maker and that he should look at me not him. I told him again that Riccardo's offer was final, turned to my computer, and started my work. Raveen then approached Riccardo and told him he could introduce several colleagues of his to us. Riccardo told him that if he introduced them and they signed for at least six months, he would remove £10 from his rent for each tenant introduced. I thought that was a good deal. Finally, Raveen kept quiet. He signed the contract and left the office like a poodle. I cannot imagine how some people think. Raveen got a fully furnished, triple room in a four-bedroom house; a weekly cleaner; unlimited Internet access; and free council tax, water, and TV licence. He got all of that and still felt as if I had just robbed him.

Within three weeks of moving in, he called Riccardo to ask him for another desk. He asked for the same desk that he had in another room in the house. I told him that the desks were exactly the same. He then complained that the leg of the desk was unstable, so I told him to bend down and screw the legs on properly. After that, he stopped moaning for a couple of days. Later, though, he asked Riccardo to put a mirror in his room. He kept calling and texting him for about a week. He explained that he needed it to tie his head turban every morning. Riccardo finally gave in and asked me to give one to him. I called Raveen and told him that if he seriously needed a mirror, he should buy one himself. I told him that there was no way I could provide everything for each tenant. Plus, he knew there was no mirror in his room before he moved in. In the end, I agreed to put a mirror in the lounge but not his room. Again, he felt like a poodle, but he was quiet for a few weeks. And then

I received a call from one of the tenants about Raveen. He refused to pay his share of the electric and gas top-up on time, was extremely dirty, and left all his dirty dishes in the kitchen sink. I told the other tenants to pack up all his dishes and place them in front of his door every time that happened. To make matters worse, he always paid late; I consistently had to remind him about his rent payment. It was not an ideal situation.

Ella

Ella was particularly bad. She found my advert on the Internet when I was just starting off in the business. I had just taken on my fourth house and was eager to rent out all the rooms as I did with the previous three houses. Ella approached me for the last room of the house. She came to me with the backing of the council and was my first contact with an LHA tenant. She came with a member of the council who wanted to ensure that the house was suitable to be rented out as a house share. I gave them the EPC certificate and the PAT on all appliances after they checked the smoke alarms. They were very happy with the state of the house and assured me that the council would pay £265 per month (Ella would pay the remaining £35). I waited for eight weeks to receive my first payment, which was not too bad.

After four months, Ella found a job. She didn't tell me, but I found out when the council stopped paying me. When I called the council, they informed me and stated that they were no longer in charge of Ella. When I called Ella, she told me that she was not able to pay because her job was not regular. Evidently, she was going to discuss the matter with the council again. She begged me to wait for a few weeks until she could get an answer from the council. She asked nicely, and because I believed her story, I waited for another month. At that time, I called the council. Again, they confirmed that they were not going to take her on board because she was earning enough to pay her rent. When I confronted her, she became very aggressive and mouthy. She told me that I could not kick her out without two months' notice. I immediately called my contact from the tenancy relations department at the council, and he told me to start the eviction procedure in order to get her out of the house. He also recommended that I take her to small claims court in order to retrieve my money. I followed his advice.

When she received the small claims letter, she immediately moved out (apparently forgetting about the two months' notice and half the stuff in her room). I immediately confiscated everything, even though there was nothing of value. I'm guessing she didn't have the space for her lamp and double bed. Still, I was happy to get my room back. The small claims court awarded me the judgement and demanded that she pay me £1100. I e-mailed her the judgement and gave her two options: pay the whole amount in full or pay me weekly when she got paid. She agreed to the latter option but never paid a penny despite my persistent calls for weeks. Finally, I decided to stick a County Court Judgment (CCJ) on her when she stopped taking my calls and e-mails. As of the time of this writing, I have not heard anything from her.

Marissa and Dan

I remember when I saw this young couple for the first time. They were with Dan's mother. She was a very nice, polite lady, but she looked trashy. I decided to give them the benefit of the doubt, though, because I was still inexperienced. Dan's mother told me that they had been looking for a place for a couple of months but most landlords did not allow couples in their house shares. I did not understand that rationale at the time. For their part, the couple seemed to love the large double room that was fully furnished with a double bed, desk, chair, wardrobe, and large sofa. They also appreciated that they only had to pay for gas and electricity. They were very happy to find a clean house with mostly English sharers. I asked the mother what she was doing for a living; she told me she was a letting agent. At the time, I had not drafted my guarantor form, so I just asked her for her address and signature as proof that she would be the guarantor for the couple.

After four months at the house, the couple started to miss payments. In fact, they only paid after receiving text reminders. On the sixth month, they called me to ask whether they could use their deposit to pay their last month's rent. I told them that that was not the way I ran my business. They then told me that I did not have a choice because they did not have any money. I told them about their outstanding bill of £278, but they decided to ignore me. I wrote them official letters, but they claimed that I needed to give them two months' notice to evict them. I had a six-month agreement with them, and the real drama began on that sixth month. I called Dan's mother, and she told me that the kids had complained to her about the mould in the room. I thought to myself, *Hold on, this is the first time I've heard anything like that! And if the room was mouldy, why can't they open the windows to ventilate it?* She said they couldn't because it was too cold outside. I was shocked. I immediately started converting our oral conversations into writing in case I needed proof in court. The couple decided not to address the situation and left me to deal with the mother, a crazy piece of trash.

By the end, I just wanted the kids out of the house the day their contract ended. When they vacated the house, however, they left a few surprises. First, they left holes in the walls. Evidently, they put up shelves, removed them, and decided not to cover the resulting holes. The room was full of trash and cider bottles. I contacted the mother and showed her the pictures, but she just said, 'Well show me the inventory you made when they came in.' Unfortunately, I was a complete novice and did not have any inventories. I had pictures that I took when the room was on the market, but I did not make them sign anything. It was my mistake. I then asked about the bill, which I was determined not to let go. When she saw the itemised bill, however, she contested it. She refused to pay because the bill looked too high. I gave her copies of the bills and the number to call if she wanted any more proof. I told her I would take the couple to court if they did not come up with a payment plan.

After a couple of months of battle, I decided to stop all contact with the mother. I wrote a long e-mail to Marissa explaining the consequences if I took them both to court. Basically, they would have to pay the amount they owed *and* all my court costs plus interest. She decided to pay £10 per week until the amount was fully repaid. The £10 quickly turned into £5 pounds, though, and after a couple of months, she stopped paying altogether. After that experience, I decided to switch all energy in my houses to pay-as-you-go. I should have done that right from the start because I no longer struggle with energy bills.

Lee

This man in his forties approached me the first day I showed my new property. It was my third house at the time. He begged me to give him one of my rooms because he had been thrown out by his ex-wife. Looking at him, I would have thrown him out before the first day!

He wanted the second smallest room in the house, which was priced at £360 (including most bills). He did not have the deposit, but he could pay the rent straight away. I decided to try a three-month contract with him. We agreed that he would pay the deposit in two instalments starting with the second month. What a great mistake that was! Remember, I was just starting off and knew nothing about human desperation. I still believed in human trustworthiness.

At the end of the first two months, I reminded him of his first instalment. I was given the excuse that he had his daughter with him and could not afford the instalment that month. He promised to start paying the following month. Because business was good and I had no reason to doubt a man older than I was who just happened to be going through a rough time with his family, I decided to give him another chance. By the time the third month arrived, all payments had stopped. He didn't pay the rent, his first gas and electricity bill, or his instalment. I went to the house and stuck the bill on the fridge as I usually did in all my houses. His share was around £84 for the three months. When I realised that he was struggling to pay the bill on top of his rent, the reality hit me. He had a full-time job and a car, but he was not prioritising the roof over his head.

One day, I made an impromptu visit to the house. I saw him drinking beer with his friends in the garden. I called him aside (so as not to embarrass him in front of his friends) and asked him for the first deposit instalment. He became mouthy. I wasn't sure whether that was the result of the alcohol, so I decided to call him the following day. We were already in the fourth month, he had not paid his monthly rent, and his trial contract was completed. On the phone, he was verbally abusive. By that time, he had forgotten about our temporary agreement, so I kindly reminded him that the tenancy had expired and that he was illegally occupying my house. He went dead quiet on the phone. I told him that I would be around the following day to collect the deposit in full or he had to move out.

I was not sure what he was going to do when I arrived, so I asked my handyman to come along with me. When we arrived, the room was completely empty. Luckily, he was kind enough to leave the keys on his desk. I could not believe it! I was thrilled that he had vacated without causing any damage to the house and left the keys. As I was leaving the house, my gut instinct told me to check on the other tenants in the house. I asked one of the guys whether he knew where Lee was, but he did not know anything. And then I went to knock on the second guy's door and asked him whether Lee had left anything behind. I was quite sure that his little car could not fit all his belongings, so I looked the guy in the eyes and asked the question again. He admitted quickly that he had his flat screen TV, speakers, CDs, and a bike. I asked him to release everything. I then took pictures of all the items and asked him to tell Lee that he could pick up his belongings once all the money owed was paid. I received a call within thirty minutes; he wanted to pay me and take his stuff back. I told him he had fourteen days to make the payment and get his stuff. He agreed but never showed up. I kept his stuff for over a month. I tried calling him, but he had changed his number. Thus, I ended up placing the TV in a new house.

Cole

Cole was introduced to me by one of my former tenants. The former tenant had a six-month contract with me. After three months, he found a job far from the house, so we agreed that he could find somebody to replace himself and get his deposit back in full. One day, he called and asked whether he could accompany his colleague, Cole, who was desperately looking for an accommodation in the area. When I met Cole, he seemed nice but emotionally scarred. He was on the brink of crying as he told me about the loss of his mother. I felt sympathetic and asked him when she died. He told me that she died about a year earlier. I was moved by his fragile state because I had lost my father around the same time. We agreed that he would move into the house as soon as the other guy left. That would give him two weeks to pay his rent and deposit in full. I was wise to take a down payment of £100 pounds that same day.

After a week, he called me to say that he was starting a new job and might not be able to pay the deposit. He did, however, assure me that there would be no problem paying the rent. He was quite honest, so I agreed to let him move in without the deposit. By that time I had had a lot of experience, including fifteen properties under my belt, so I knew I was making a mistake. Nevertheless, I still fell for his cat like meows! I knew it was unwise, but I let him into my house. After the first month, on the day his rent was due, he called me to ask whether he could pay weekly because he was paid weekly. I saw no problem with that. I told him that, as long as he paid, I had no issue with him.

He paid me the first week, but neglected to do so the second week. When I called, he told me he would pay the following Friday. And when the following Friday came, he paid just half of the money, promising to pay the rest on Monday. Monday came, but I heard no news from Cole. I called him endlessly until I finally reached him. He told me that he was expecting some money from his family and even showed me the proof of transfer from his family. I was stupid to believe he was telling the truth. The day he was supposed to receive the money arrived, but Cole did not show up. His phone was off for the next two days. I decide to visit the house one day at ten o'clock at night. I knew I would catch him then. Unsurprisingly, he was playing video games on my TV. You should have seen the shock on his face! I got my money that evening. Things went back to normal for a while, but then I received a call from one of the tenants who explained that Cole had been housing a guest for the past couple of weeks, which was against my house rules. I confronted him about the matter, and he said it was a temporary situation. I asked him to remove his guest immediately. And then the late payments started again. After three months, I could no longer tolerate him—he was a compulsive and mouthy liar.

Whenever I asked for my payment, he either lied or verbally abused me. As a result, I decided to give him notice to leave. On the day he was supposed to leave, I received a text from him asking me for another week. I agreed. When that date came, he told me he had moved out but needed another week to collect the rest of his stuff. By that time, my skin was numb: my handyman and I went to his room and packed his stuff. One of the tenants called him about the situation, and he immediately called me back. I told him he could pick up his stuff from my office as long as he brought the outstanding rent. I separated his valuable things, which I kept safely inside my locked office room and put the rest of his stuff near the entrance of my office. At eleven o'clock at night, he called me several times, but I could not be bothered to pick up the phone. The following day, when I got to the office, his stuff at the entrance was gone. My tenants in my office maisonette had opened the door and allowed him to take his stuff. I was furious but relieved that I still had his precious things in my office room. I texted him to collect his belongings, but he never replied. After about two months, though, he called me. We agreed to meet at the office so he could collect his things as long as he paid his outstanding debt. He never showed up. A few days later, I saw him in a bar; he was in the back garden with friends, smoking weed. Curiously, he could not afford to pay his rent, but he could buy weed.

Henry

I did not personally meet Henry when he moved into my house. At that stage, I was doing fewer viewings because I had two other people taking care of that part of the business for me. Basically, I was spending a lot more time in the office taking care of administrative tasks. I was told that Henry was a nice chap who needed a cheap room for a couple of months. It was November, and the business was consequently entering the quiet Christmas period. The room he wanted was a single room with a single bed, a small desk, a chair, and a rail for hanging his clothes. I asked for £200, most bills included. The room was in a big house with a lounge, a massive kitchen, two bathrooms, and two gardens. The house was very spacious, which is why I did not mind renting out the smallest room.

I saw Henry around two weeks after he moving in. He was about six feet four inches tall and approximately twenty stones. I could not understand how he could contain himself in such a small room with a single bed.

When I saw him, I asked him to confirm that he would be staying at the house for just a couple of months, which he did. When he moved in, he paid his monthly rent but just £100 of his deposit. I usually charge £100 if a tenants wants to stay for fewer than three months. When the second month arrived, however, Henry did not pay his rent. When I called him, he told me he would make a weekly payment starting from Monday, which was just a couple of days away. I then informed him again that I would be closing down his room soon because I needed it as storage for the rest of the house. He was confused and said, 'Okay, I will move out if that is what you want.' I told him the agreement was for him to stay just a couple of months, not eternally.

Over the course of the next four weeks, it was a struggle to get his weekly rent from him. In addition to that, he started smoking in the room, the lounge, and the kitchen. When I told him it was forbidden, he apologised as if it were the first time I confronted him about the matter. He asked me for a new mattress a week before he was supposed to move out because the other one was hurting his back. You can imagine my face when I received that request. He was not making his payments, he was smoking in the house, and he was incredibly dirty—all that, and he had the balls to request a new mattress a week before his agreed departure day. I told him to get lost.

When the day of his departure arrived, he called my colleague to tell him that he was not moving out because he had nowhere else to go. He then told me that the council informed him that I had to give him two months' notice anyway. I spoke with my contact at the council, and he told me that my mistake was not giving him a notice to quit when he moved in to ensure that he left at the end of the agreed term. Thus, I had to put up with the parasite for another two months. All the other tenants at the house were fed up with him. When they heard that he was staying for another two months, they all handed in their notices. After a month, the other good tenants left the whole house to Henry, the only one who never paid. I confronted him once more and he told me that, after viewing my website, he had decided not to be a part of my route to success. He said he was not going to pay a penny for the room.

And that was that: I was going to be losing £1300 a month because of him. Obviously, though, I didn't want to let that happen. Luckily for me, a university called me after seeing my advert somewhere. They wanted to send four engineers to live in the same house because no other landlords in the area had a suitable house for them. Luckily, I had Henry's house available, and there were exactly four rooms free. They moved in within days, saving me from the loss. Was Henry happy about that? Of course not. He wanted to make sure that they left the house like the previous tenants. Thus, he decided to take his dirtiness to the next level. He used the toilet, messed it all up, and left it for the next person to clean. The new tenants, from Germany, France, and Spain were not used to that kind of filth. They started to complain the moment they moved in. I said to myself, *This is not happening again!* I told them that he would be gone in two weeks. I made it clear when I gave Henry the two-month notice that I would not tolerate him in the house a minute more than two months.

When the last day arrived, he told me he had moved out. I went to the house and found some of his belongings still lingering in the room. I took out my plastic gloves and started amassing the objects in black bins. I called my handyman to change the locks and texted Henry to let him know that his belongings would be placed outside the house for his collection. He was fuming on the phone; he said I had no right to kick him out. He said he had spoken with the council and the shelter who told him that I could not force him out. Remember: I had no contract with him at that time and he was not paying a penny of his rent. I told him to go back to the shelter and the council and tell them to lodge him. He needed to be someone else's problem from that point forward. He was an English, full-grown man of twenty-seven. He had blonde hair and blue eyes and could have been a successful gigolo because he had the looks. Instead, he was a lazy parasite.

The following day, after packing and changing the locks, he tried to enter the room while the other tenants were sleeping. It was about one o'clock in the morning when he started knocking on the door, climbing on the roof, and looking for access into the house. Unfortunately, he found a way in. He climbed through the roof window of one of the bathrooms. He had a girl with him; I think he was looking for a place to sleep with her. They were both very drunk. Luckily for me, I had removed the bed from the room, so there was nothing but carpet for him. Plus, I had locked the lounge room to prevent anyone from sleeping on the couches. When he saw that there was nowhere to do his business, he simply opened the door from the inside and walked out with his companion. I texted him the following morning concerning his actions. I explained that trespassing was a criminal offence. I then told him to turn up at two o'clock in the afternoon to collect his stuff.

I was waiting for him in front of the house, and he looked like a little cat when he turned up. His two hands were not big enough to carry his stuff, so he asked whether he could come back. I told him to get lost. He then said, 'This is all pretty unnecessary.' I shut the door in his face. That was the last time I saw him. I believe he still roams around the area. Some members of my team see him now and again acting as if nothing ever happened.

One would think that, after all the experiences I've outlined thus far, I would have learned something when it comes to picking a tenant. I have to say that the bad tenants call me *the bitch*. No matter how much I know about tenant behaviour, I still let in another parasite every now and then. I have to say that 97 per cent of my tenants are fantastic people who always pay on time and take care of my houses; 2 per cent are very bad, and 1 per cent are ugly. The bad and ugly ones tend to ruin the mood that the good ones leave behind. Henry was bad but not the worst. The worst ones in my book are Davies and a couple, Alfa and Charmeen.

Davies

Davies first came to view a house of mine in another area. I was the one who did the viewing. When I saw him, I knew he was trouble. He looked like another parasite, so I immediately requested a guarantor, a proof of employment, a proof of income, etc. That was the last I saw of him until a few weeks later when I noticed that he had been signed on by a member of my team. He had provided all the necessary papers; everything looked good. Still, gut instinct plays a part in this game.

When I saw Davies again, I remembered him and thought to myself, *Here is one that slipped through the net.* I knew that I was in for a long ride, so I immediately instated a structure. I indicated that all our communication should be in writing. At that stage, my team and I only signed three-month trial contracts. If someone did not behave correctly, we sent a notice that we wouldn't renew the contract within the first month and give the tenant two months' notice to leave.

Davies paid his first months' rent and deposit as requested. He provided the requisite paperwork, and nothing was wrong until two weeks later. Evidently, he broke the lounge window by opening it from the top, causing it to crash down. He texted me that same evening. I went to look at it the following morning. When I asked what happened, the Hispanic tenants explained the situation. I told Davies that he was responsible for the window. The window was not supposed to be pulled in that manner, and someone with decent common sense would know it might come crashing down. When I informed him of the situation, he showed his true character. I knew I was in for a good ride. Davies was an experienced parasite, and I knew he would use all the loopholes in the law to stay in the house. My main objective was to get him out at the end of the three-month trial. I immediately gave him his two-month notice and informed him that I would not renew his contract at the end of the agreed term. I assumed he would stop paying his rent and that I had to accept losing a months' rent if he left on time. I also started a small claims court action against him. And as I guessed, he stopped paying his rent when it was due.

I wanted to make sure that the court sent him the paperwork before he left, so I searched the Internet to learn how to take someone to small claims court. I landed at the following website: https://www.moneyclaim.gov.uk/web/mcol/welcome. This website took me through the process step by step. I paid the £66 fee to put down my claim and printed out the proof of claim. Here, I must emphasise that I tried everything in my power to avoid legal action. I went that route only because Davies refused to pay his rent and the cost of the window.

When he received the letter from the small claims court, he said he would leave if I gave his deposit back. I agreed. But then he said it was an empty threat, that he did not expect me to agree to those terms. Of course, he had nowhere to go, though, so the drama went on for another month. Luckily for me, he packed his bags at the end of the third month. After two months, the court sent us both a letter indicating that we should appear at Bristol Court. I went with all my records and paperwork. Davies did not show up. Thus, Davies had to pay his rent, the cost of the window, the court costs, and interest within a few weeks. No surprise, he never did. Consequently, I awarded him a CCJ, which will affect his credit rating for the next six years. From my experience, I learned to request not only an employer's reference and guarantor, but also a copy of a payslip or NI number. If I ever come across an individual like him again, I will request an *attachment of earnings,* which will pay me via the person's future earnings.

After a year, while walking to my office, I came across Davies. I did not recognise him at first. He had a beard and looked like a tramp. When I finally realised who he was, I asked for my money. Of course, he ran off like the thief that he is.

Alfa and Charmeen

I read once in an online horoscope that people who fall under the Sagittarius sign are more drawn towards human sufferings. As a Sagittarius, that sounds right to me. I am always drawn towards helping others and giving them the benefit of the doubt, even when my gut instinct tells me to stay away.

When I met Alfa, he looked roughly decent. By that, I mean he looked rough, but his words were decent. He told me he had a job, which I verified. He told me where he worked, and I happened to have another tenant who worked at the same place, so that was fine. And then he told me that he would be living with his girlfriend, Charmeen. I asked to meet her before letting them both into the house. He informed me that Charmeen had found a job close to the house but needed to go through a month of induction and various checks before being given a permanent contract. They had payment for the first month, but they asked to pay the deposit bit by bit over the coming months. I agreed because they looked stranded, young, and promising. Alfa looked into my eyes and told me that he would always pay weekly, on Fridays, unless he was busy (in which case, he explained, he would pay on Mondays). I told him that was fine as long as he informed me in advance and stuck to his dates. I decided to lock them into a three-month agreement, and I also made him sign a notice to quit at that time. If things did not work out, he had to leave at the end of the agreement without delay.

The first four weeks were fine because he paid me in advance when they moved in. During the second month, however, irregularities cropped up. He called to inform me that his Friday payment was going to be late and that he would pay on Monday. After hounding him, he finally paid on Wednesday. When the second Friday came around, the same thing happened. And the third Friday was accompanied by the same drama. I told him that he could not afford the room and needed to find something cheaper. He begged me to let him stay, explaining that he was having problems with Charmeen, who was now living with her mother. I called Charmeen to ask whether she was still living in the house, and she confirmed that she had moved out.

Alfa agreed to downgrade to a smaller, cheaper room of mine, which became available at the same time. He was going to be paying just £300 per month instead of £435. When I showed him the room, we agreed that it was just for him—I did not want another couple in the house. After two weeks, the couple living in the house moved out and Alfa called immediately to ask whether he and Charmeen could move into the new room. I refused the request. I was certain he could not afford the rent even though it was only £370. They both begged me and confirmed that they were both working and could pay the rent. After numerous calls and begging, I finally agreed to let them move into the bigger room. Within a week, they moved in and started disturbing the neighbourhood with loud music. When I spoke with them, they agreed to be more considerate. And then the fighting started. They beat one another like animals, screaming and shouting in the middle of the night. Sometimes, the neighbours called the police. When I was informed of the situation, I decided that the couple had to go.

At that time, my older tenants in the house started to complain. Clearly, I didn't want to lose the valuable tenants to accommodate two pieces of shit. Plus, they couldn't make their weekly payments on time. Unbeknown to me, they made a copy of the key to their former house so they could collect their mail there. Apparently, they were waiting for a very important letter. When I confronted them about the situation, they denied everything (even though one of the tenants in the other house saw them). I told them that their three-months trial was coming up and that they had to leave at that point. They agreed, but unsurprisingly, they broke that promise, too. They asked for another week, and I allowed them to stay because I wanted them to leave peacefully. I informed them that I needed all my furniture from the room because the new tenants wanted the room empty before they moved in.

Of course, when move-out day arrived, they were still in the house. As I entered the house, I saw both of them. They were not happy and scared about what I was going to do. I proceeded to collect my furniture, and with my handyman's help, changed the entrance lock. Alfa was furious and nearly ready to fight. He whispered into my ear that he would stab me if he ever came across me. I immediately called the police, and they arrived within ten minutes. I told them what was happening, and they asked me to wait outside while they spoke with the couple. Remember: they were no longer paying rent and constantly disturbing the neighbourhood, so the police had a few records on them already. I do not know what went on inside, but within twenty-four hours, they had moved out of my house and left the keys in the bedroom. Nothing was damaged. I proceeded to change the locks and all seemed well.

A few days later, however, I went to their first house to collect letters. While there, I saw a few letters for them. I accidentally opened one from a debt collector company. I called them, told them about the mail, and wished them good luck. And then I opened another letter that was addressed to me. The letter was asking me to provide references for them. Really!? They gave a landlord my name to get a reference? Really? Life is a bitch! I called the number on the piece of paper and did not hold my tongue.

Kev

When I met Kev, he looked like a decent man. Indeed, he was a decent man—he always paid on time. I created a three-month contract for him. He was the first tenant in a new, four-bedroom house I had just taken on my books. I told him that, because he was the first tenant, he would see us doing viewings of the other rooms. I told him we would try to do them when he was at work or give him twenty-four hours' notice. He was fine with that. We rented out two rooms within days of renting to Kev; the last room took some time, however. In fact, we had to keep doing viewings for three weeks. We scheduled the viewings while he was normally at work to stay out of his way because I knew he was a bit twitchy about seeing us around. One night, at ten o'clock, I received a call from someone who was highly interested in the room. He wanted to view the place and move in the following day. Thus, I immediately texted everyone in the house to inform them of the viewing, which would take place at six o'clock in the evening the following day (Kev usually came back from work at five o'clock). When I sent the text, everyone else was okay with the viewing except Kev. He explained that he would be in the house and that I didn't give him twenty-four hours' notice. I then offered to do the viewing at ten o'clock, but he did not reply so I went ahead with my plans.

When I got there, Kev was at the door but wouldn't allow me to come in. Because that was my first experience with that kind of behaviour, I just pushed the door open and let myself and the viewer into the house. I proceeded to do my viewing while Kev followed us and told me that he did not want the room to be rented because he did not want to live with more than two people. That was a first for me. I turned around and told him that he needed to take a house by himself if he didn't want to live in a house share. I tried my best to keep my calm and proceed with the viewing. When we arrived in the lounge, which led to the back garden, my guest stepped outside into the garden. I followed him outside to show him the small hallway that led from the front of the house and into the back garden. He needed a safe place to park his bike without having to bring it through the house. The house was simply perfect for him.

When I stepped outside of the garden, however, I found out that Kev had been following us and locked the garden door behind us. Thus, we couldn't get back inside through the garden. We walked around the house to go through the front door, but he had locked it and situated himself in front so I couldn't push it open. I proceeded to call the other guys in the house, but unfortunately for me, only the skinniest guy was at home. I told my guest that I had never seen such a thing in my entire life. I apologised because he had come all the way from Swansea to view the room, but didn't get the chance to see it. He left disappointed and told me that he wouldn't want to live with Kev even if the room and the house were perfect. I went straight back to the office, typed up Kev's non-renewal contract and informed him of his last day in the house. The letter was hand delivered.

After the event, I was unable to do any viewings in the house. In that span of time, I received a call from a young man from Kazakhstan who needed a room for a couple of months. He had seen my advert and noted that the house was close to his school. He took the room the same day. He got a friend of his to pay me by transfer and arrived two days later. Luckily for me, Kev was not in the house at the time. I explained the situation to him, and he told me in his cute accent, 'Don't you worry, I can take him on.' The guy was a bodybuilder and looked like a Russian bodyguard one might see in the Kremlin. I texted everyone that same day to inform them that the last room had been rented and the new occupants was happily settled. I wish I could have seen Kev's face when he saw the new tenant that evening. I called the new guy the following day to see whether anything had happened, but he told me the night was uneventful. He introduced himself to everyone that evening and got along with all of them. I told him to keep me posted if anything happened.

A couple of days later, I received a call from the council. They wanted to inspect the house because they had received a call from Kev stipulating that the house was overcrowded. I told them that there were four bedrooms with four tenants, a lounge, a bathroom, a toilet, and two gardens. They wanted to see the house for themselves, though, so we arranged a day and time. When they arrived, Kev was with them. The lady looked around, turned to Kev, and said, 'there is nothing wrong here.' She apologised, and in short order, we became the best of friends. She is now one of my contacts at the council.

On the day Kev was supposed to leave, I went to the house, but the room was empty. He had steam-cleaned the room, dusted the window, left my keys, and paid his outstanding bills. I couldn't believe it! I think he was bipolar.

David and Alice

These tenants were afflicted with this-is-still-my-house syndrome. They had spent many months in the house without incident, but then became unbearable for the last month of their stay. When they moved out, they realised that they still needed my cooperation in order to get all their mail back. But because they had burned the bridge between us, they decided to ask the new tenants directly for their mail.

Normally, good tenants are expected to adhere to the rules and regulations stipulated in the agreement. For instance, good tenants can't leave without cleaning their rooms. There is usually a £50 charge for us to clean for them, and that sum is usually subtracted from their deposit. Of course, they are often very unhappy about any money taken from their deposit. This animosity causes some tenants to refuse to pay for the gas and electricity top-up during the last week. I usually call the other tenants at the house if there are any outstanding top-up charges before I return the deposit. And if there are any charges, I deduct them from the deposit. Also, I usually ask the current tenants whether the leaving tenant broke anything while he or she was living in the house. Despite an inventory, it is hard to know these things without asking. If the leaving tenant is responsible for any broken items that belong to the house, he or she will have to pay for it.

We get threats all the time when a tenant thinks he or she is more clever than we are and can get away with something. For example, I had a tenant called Chris who stayed in one of my rooms for five months. His initial contract was for three months, but he decided to stay a bit longer, which was all right. He gave me his one-month notice, in line with our agreement. When the day arrived, my assistant tried to contact him to arrange an exit inventory, but we heard nothing from him. Consequently, she decided to go to the house and see for herself. (We had to have the room ready for the new tenant who was moving in the same afternoon.) When we got there, the room was empty and cleaned except for some rubbish bags he left behind.

Because the house had pay-as-you-go gas and electricity, we often refunded the deposit within a week of the tenant departing from the house. A few days after the deposit was sent over, we heard from Chris— he wanted an additional three days' worth of rent returned. We asked him why, and he told us that he had moved out three days before the date he had given us. I could barely contain my astonishment. I asked him why he thought he should get a penny back given the fact that we were never alerted and only gained access to the house from the date he gave us. He then told us to ask the current tenants, explaining that they would confirm the exact day he departed. I told him that that was not the point. The point was that we were unable to start the new tenancy three days earlier because he had not given us that date. It was a case of a formerly good tenant turning bad. He threatened to contact the council, and I asked him whether he needed their number. I never heard from him after that.

Eron

Eron was one of my first tenants. He was with me before all my gas and electricity became a pay-as-you-go system. In fact, he was with me for over a year. He was not a good person morally, but he almost always paid on time. When I changed all the meters to pay-as-you-go at his house, the bills were so high that most of the tenants could not pay. I asked the energy company to add the debt to the meters. In other words, £6 was deducted weekly until the debt was fully paid off. All the tenants paid for almost six months until the debt was cleared. Eron, however, thought that he still had to pay his bill. I never bothered him with it, though, so he may have assumed I forgot about it.

All my tenants have to give me a month's notice before they leave; that is my golden rule. If a notice is not given, they lose their deposit. The reasoning is that it takes me time to find a replacement. When it was time for Eron to pay his rent, he was nowhere to be found. I knew he travelled a lot for his work, so I figured that he was out of the country. I called his number and sent him several e-mails, but I didn't receive any response. After ten days, I went to the house to see whether he was still there. Surprisingly, he had taken off and left me with a huge mess to clean. He left the bill I had given him seven months earlier on the table. I sent him a final e-mail telling him it was stupid to lose a deposit in that manner. Had he given me a month's notice, as stipulated in the contract, he would have gotten his entire deposit back because the whole house had finished paying for the energy bills through the top-ups anyway. He had no reason to run away like a thief. I never heard anything back, though. I later found about a dozen letters from debt collectors and small loan companies requesting payments. Evidently, he took out thousands of pounds worth of loans from various companies and did the runner. I hope they catch him.

Jakub and Evelina

As I said earlier, most of my bad experiences took place when I had just started my Rent2Rent strategy. I met Jacob and Anna when I still believed strongly in helping anyone who came my way. They both contacted me asking for a room for a couple. I happened to be advertising one at the time, so I decided to give them a go for three months. They told me that Jacob was working in a factory and that Anna was looking for a job. That didn't strike me as atypical. They asked me whether they could do some work around the house in exchange for reduced rent. Again, that was not unusual. I regularly used my tenants to maintain the gardens and clean the houses if they asked me for a reduced rent. In fact, I prefer that situation. So when they asked me what needed to be done in the house, I told them that they could maintain the front and back gardens and clean the house weekly for a reduced rent. They were very happy with that idea. I was also happy about the deal; after all, I needed the grass to be cut regularly.

After two months, they started to have money issues, even though they were being charged £350 for a large room, most bills included. There was nothing that cheap on the market, and they knew they had a good thing going. Nevertheless, they became very arrogant. Once they learned that Anna was expecting a baby, they acted as if they were untouchable. One day, I called Jacob for his rent, which was to be paid weekly, per his request. He told me that he did not have the money and explained that, because I had many houses, I could afford to let them live there for free. He also informed me that Anna was expecting a child and that I should leave them alone. I could not believe what I was hearing. I immediately drafted a notice to leave and hand delivered it. I stipulated in the letter that my houses were unsuitable for children and that I was not responsible for impregnating his girlfriend. She was his responsibility, not mine. I gave them two months to leave.

They were not happy about my decision, so they called the council. The council contacted me and asked whether I had given them two months' notice. I said, 'Yes,' and that was the end of it for them. I advised Jacob to approach the council for an accommodation, but they told him to find a private accommodation because they had over 14,000 people on their waiting list. By that time, the relationship between us had completely broken down. They were stranded, but I stayed firm on my decision to see them leave at the end of the notice. The next thing I heard was that they had found another house share with another landlord, but they were paying a lot more than they paid at my place. It worked out well because it was clearly written in the contract that children and pets were not allowed in the house.

Kacie

What does one get when one has a deeply depressed drug addict as a tenant? One gets Kacie. I knew something was wrong when she came to see me, but my knowledge about the behaviour of drug addicts was not great at that point in time. I had never been around addicts; therefore, I misinterpreted her sniffing as a cold. Kacie came along with an elderly woman whom I thought was a colleague. I later learned that she was her social worker. They saw the house and loved it because it had a bath.

Apparently, taking baths was the only thing Kacie could not do without. She had to have one every day to calm her nerves. I should have sensed that something was wrong, but I just assumed it was a strange habit. I then thought about the water bill: if the house were metered, I would have been in deep trouble.

Anyway, she was accompanied by a lady called Dita. Kacie wanted to take the room with her boyfriend, who was a building contractor. She gave me all the paperwork I asked for, including a guarantor's form. Everything looked perfect on paper. The couple moved in within a week, and everything was beautiful for about two weeks. One day, one of the previous tenants, an Italian engineer, called me to report that since Kacie had moved in with her boyfriend, the house had been thrown into chaos. They constantly fought with each other, and they were drunk or stoned most of nights. I said to myself, *You knew something was wrong and did nothing to stop it. It's all your fault.* My informant was kind enough to alert me to the situation, so I immediately told him that I only gave them a short tenancy as a trial and would not be renewing it. He was glad to hear that. I called Kacie to my office and complained about her behaviour; she apologised and told me it would not happen again. I reminded her that they only had a three-months tenancy, and if they caused any more trouble, they would be asked to leave.

I then contacted Dita, the elderly lady, and spoke with her. She told me the truth about their relationship. She told me she was her support worker and was trying to get her clean. She also mentioned that Kacie had serious personal challenges. I was quite sympathetic with her and kindly advised her to stay close to her because I didn't want any trouble. I kindly gave her the notice of non-renewal of contract. All I had to do was wait for the time to elapse and hope that nothing bad would happen before then. Things did not go the way I planned. A few weeks later, I heard that Kacie's boyfriend had broken up with her. She went downhill after that, leaving me to cope with the consequences.

I received endless calls from the other tenants regarding her habit of bringing strange men into her room. They had parties, drank, got stoned, and fought like animals. This all happened during the second month of the tenancy, and two out of the three good tenants had decided to move out because of her. I only had Kacie and another guy in the house. In short, I was losing money; Kacie had to leave. I was helpless, though: I hated her, but I could not do anything but wait till she left. One night, as I was driving past the house, I saw a police car parked in front of the house. I thought she might have harmed herself, but luckily for me, she was just drunk. Apparently, the police were simply dropping her off at the house.

Her departure day finally arrived. I was at the house very early; one would have thought I was waiting for Father Christmas to arrive. I made sure that she was not going to change her mind. Dita had previously asked me whether she could stay a little longer, to which I responded, 'No!' I was as patient as I could be, but I just could not stand her any longer. I did not want to see her or hear her or smell her. I just wanted her to leave. They packed all their stuff but left a large drawer behind. They needed to pick it up the following day. I told them to be at the house at 9:00 in the morning—sharp—or the drawer would be left at the front door. They came to pick it up as arranged. Dita apologised later for what had happened. I told her that she should not impose such a liability on other landlords, no matter how much she wanted to rehabilitate an addict. I explained that landlords need to know what they are taking on. She told me that she wished things could have been different. At that stage, I was at my boiling point but wished her all the best. Kacie was no longer my problem.

Jorge and Samia

The last string of bad tenants was a Hispanic couple who seemed to think that being in a house share was like being in a hotel or serviced apartment. I remember being at one of my networking events when I met a gentleman called Estefano. He was a Hispanic landlord in one of the towns near my home. We were talking about the volume of Hispanic folks arriving in Bristol every month. I think I read in a newspaper that the figure was around one thousand arrivals each month. Estefano then warned me about the tenant/Landlord laws in Spain. He then told me the story of his houses in Spain. According to him, the laws in Spain gave too many rights to the tenants and too few to the landlords. He warned me about the demands and expectations bound up with the Hispanic market. I took his advice but informed him that, thus far, my troublesome tenants had been born and bred in England. But then I met Jorge and Samia.

The best word to describe this couple is *delusional.* The couple were the first to move into a newly acquired, five-bedroom property. They took the biggest room of the house—one could fit two standard doubles in it. We informed them that, hopefully, the house would be filled very quickly because it was in a very good location. The house was just a ten-minute walk to the city centre and a two-minute walk to one of the largest supermarkets in the area. They were very happy with everything. Within a couple of days, we rented three more rooms in the house, leaving just one room before the house would be closed. In my experience, the longer it takes to fill a house, the worse the relationship will be between the tenants who already live there and me. That is reason why we tend to give ourselves only a week to close the book. It works most of the time, but in some cases, it takes longer (especially if the current tenants are filthy). Indeed, it took us three weeks to find a suitable tenant for the last room because the others were filthy.

When new tenants move into one of my houses, I usually show them how everything works inside and outside the house. My main concern is the rubbish management, which could be something new for foreigners. I showed the tenants the correct way to manage their rubbish so that the garbage men would never refuse to collect their bags. I explain that the system in the United Kingdom is pretty regimented and requires one to stick to the system. Also, I generally change the gas and electricity system during the first few weeks and explain how it works. For these tenants, however, the change of habit was daunting. Jorge was an intern at a company, but he was not getting paid much money. Samia stayed at home most of the day watching the paint dry. When we detected that behaviour, we became concerned about the implications. When someone does not work and spends all of his or her time in the house, he or she usually searches for faults in the house.

One day, as I was driving past the house, I saw a mountain of rubbish bags and food waste scattered in front of the house. I stopped my car and knocked on the door. Samia appeared, and I asked her what was going on with the rubbish. She told me that she did not know what was going on. I asked her whether she and the rest of tenants knew the rules, and she said that the other tenants were to blame. I told her that we were both going to clean up the mess, right there and then. I went back to my car, took out a pair of rubber gloves, and proceeded to clean the front garden with Samia. Again, I explained how to separate food garbage from plastic garbage and other matters.

Some weeks later, I started receiving complaints from another tenant in the house regarding the stream of strangers staying at the house. Some cultures, especially the hot countries, tend to stay together. They always want to stay as a group and party all night. This doesn't cause any harm, but it might disturb the neighbours. I do not mind visitors coming to the houses as long as I do not receive any complaint from either the other tenants or the neighbours. In this case, I started to receive calls from the other tenants. On top of that, the rubbish started to pile up because no one in the house remember to put the bags out.

I arranged a meeting at the house to speak with everyone. At the meeting, I recognised the hatred among the tenants. The three Hispanics were against the Nigerian and the British guys. They were divided into two clans, and they decided to make each other's lives hell. The Hispanics brought friends and relatives into the house and refused to top-up extra gas and electricity. So the two other guys had to pay double their weekly budget. To retaliate, the two guys stopped communicating with the Hispanics. I asked why the rubbish was pilling up in the house, and each clan blamed the other. All I could see was that they all refused to clean the house and top-up the gas and electricity. For weeks, they did not have power. I had never seen something like that before. At that point, I told them that, as soon as their tenancies ran out, I would not renew any of them. The Hispanics decided to leave early, and I was quite happy about that. I told them that they needed to clean up the whole house if they wanted to see their deposits returned. They asked me what would happen if they only cleaned their rooms and not outside the house. I told them that they would still have to pay for the cost to bring someone else in to do it. They were surprised. I was surprised that they were surprised—baffled really!

We had a couple of weeks to start organising our viewings for the next tenants. Whenever we brought in people to see the house, they were turned off by the state of the front and back gardens. Luckily for us, we did not have to do too many viewings before all three rooms were snatched off the market. After four viewings, all three rooms were taken. We had to explain the behaviour of the old tenants to the new tenants. At that stage, I still didn't know which clan was telling the truth, which clan was not cleaning up its mess.

The day the Hispanic people left the house, I inspected the house. To my huge surprise, the whole house was left untouched. The rubbish pile was bigger, and the back garden storage was full of rubbish. The two wheelie bins were overflowing, and the food waste was full of maggots and flies. The rubbish in the garden was so voluminous that the entrance to the drains was blocked, causing the flow to run into the garden.

I called my cleaner and asked for a quote. She told me it would cost £200 to do the job inside and outside the house. I texted every one of them and told them what the cost was going to be. The Hispanics immediately called me back to complain, but I just hung up on them and blocked their numbers. I had wasted so much time trying to explain the importance of taking care of the house they all lived in. Now they had to pay for their mistakes; it was only fair. My cleaner spent over six hours in the house. Sixteen large, black bins were removed by the council. She had never seen anything like it.

After the twenty-eight-day cooling off period, we returned all the deposits, minus the cost to clean up the house. It came to about £36 per person, a fair price for the amount of work that the cleaner had to do. Instead of being thankful, the Hispanic people decided to create mayhem. They decided to post on the Hispanic forums to tarnish my online reputation. The extent of their stupidity was mind-blowing; they even decided to post pictures of the house to show how dirty it was. They blamed me for it. I just could not believe it. I responded to their posts to defend myself, but the clash of culture and common sense was too great. Thus, I opted to bring in my good Hispanic tenants and other Spanish-speaking business people I knew to bring some sense into the posts. To cut a long story short, their attempts failed dramatically. My

Hispanic contacts smoked them and blasted them into outer space. They shut up after that.

Lloyd

I met Lloyd at the beginning of my adventure in property management. I posted my advert online and was contacted by his mother, a lovely lady. She explained that she was calling on behalf of her son, who was a part-time student and a part-time kitchen assistant. She and her ex-husband, Lloyd's father, were happy to be the guarantors. They offered before I even asked; I thought it was odd but rather kind.

We completed the paperwork as standard, and Lloyd moved in as planned. Everything was rosy until I started receiving calls from the other tenants regarding his parties. I have to point out that Lloyd was twenty-one back then, the youngest in the house. He would invite all his mates to chill in the house for days. It was so severe that the other paying tenants were not allowed access into the sitting room. They put up with him for about a week before informing me. When I spoke with him, he promised to stop. But of course, he did not change. I went to the house to catch him and give him a written warning advising him to entertain his friends away from the house. And then I contacted his mother, who seemed to be the only person who could handle him. At that point, he fell in line.

After about two months, the parties started again. He also decided to move his girlfriend into his single room. Two people were sleeping in the single bed. I was again informed by the tenants that she was enjoying the house. I decided to speak with Lloyd once again, but he just told me to piss off. When I went to the house to deliver his final notice, I met his girlfriend. She was enjoying the lounge, and I told her that it was time for her to leave. I explained that I would come back the following day and make her leave immediately if she had not vacated the area. She told me she would leave, and she respected her words. A few weeks later, Lloyd started to break pretty much everything in the house. He brought his bike indoors and left marks on the doors and walls. He punched his door when he was angry and slammed the entrance door when he came in at night, waking up everyone in the house. I started to receive complaints once again from the rest of the house. On top of that, he refused to clean up after using the kitchen or toilet. I knew it was time for me to give him his notice.

I contacted his mother and explained to her that her son was too young to live in a professional accommodation. I explained all that had been happening, and she apologised profusely. I gave him two months' notice. He was fine with that, and for a while, things cooled off.

One month before he left, I was informed by another tenant that Lloyd was so angry that he rammed his head into his door. He suspected that he might have put a hole in the door. I decided to do a quick inspection, so I sent him a letter informing him of my plans. When the day of the inspection came, I went into the house and into his room. Everything was tidy, but I knew what I was looking for. I was once told by a landlord that when tenants start putting up posters, they are likely hiding something. Lloyd's walls were covered in posters. I proceeded to carefully remove them one by one to check whether there were any surprises. The biggest poster was stuck on his door. I took it off and found a huge hole. It looked like he had knocked his head through it. No wonder his coconut was off the rail! I took pictures of my findings, wrote him an official letter, and requested that he replace the door within the next ten days. A copy was sent to his mother and father. Both parents responded to me by apologising for their son's behaviour and promising to fix the door. I told them that they needed to buy a new one, so I sent them the measurements and specifications.

The day he was supposed to move arrived. Both parents were there. They replaced the door on that day; they knew that he would have broken it again had they replaced it earlier. We exchanged contracts, completed the waiver form, and left each other happily. After about three months, I received a call from his mother. She wanted to know whether I would consider housing her son. She explained that Lloyd was living in a student house and his life was miserable. He wanted to return to a mature house, but no landlord would take him on. I told her that I was not prepared to have him back; he needed to grow up a little bit more. She understood my point, thanked me, and never contacted me again.

Max

There is something about young men who need their mothers to stand up for them. There might be something psychologically wrong when this happens. I say this because, all the times that I have dealt with a mother, I have had a problem with the tenant. The good thing is, mothers are often the peacemakers who resolve problems. Max's mother contacted me and was extremely nice on the phone. We spoke for at least twenty minutes as we exchanged information. I gathered that she just wanted her son out of the house. He was probably driving her crazy. She asked me whether her son could move in the following day, and I told her that it was possible as long as all the references came back fine and she filled out the lengthy guarantor's form on time. I was quite suspicious of his situation though, so I chose to go with a three-months contract.

With all the paperwork in place, Max moved into the house the following day. Everything was fine for a few weeks. I told the mother that I needed to see how he got along with the rest of the house. After a few weeks, my cleaner started to complain about the mess in the kitchen. Plates were piling up and there was always water left standing around the sink and on the floor. I went to investigate the matter. I then met one of the two girls living in the house. She explained to me that Max was the filthiest man she had ever met. No wonder his mother wanted him out of her house! She explained that, whenever he washed his dishes, he nearly flooded the kitchen. I do not know how that is possible, but that's what happened. Thus, I decided to speak with him in a very professional way. I explained that he might cause damage if he did not wipe off the water after washing up. He looked at me as if I were not even talking to him. Before leaving, I thought, *That's very odd!*

A few days later, I received several calls within a few minutes from the girls living in the house. They explained that Max was threatening and bullying them. I thought that was very odd because Max seemed more like a shy person who couldn't even look into a girl's eyes. I figured the girls were exaggerating. The following day, when my cleaner went to do her weekly cleaning, Max lashed out at her. Apparently she was disturbing his sleep at ten o'clock in the morning. My cleaner called after her job was finished to tell me what had just happened. I had no reason to doubt her or the other girls at that stage. Unfortunately for Max, my cleaner's partner was also my handyman—a strong, bold, muscular Hungarian man. When he heard about what his girlfriend had just been through, he immediately called me. He was fuming! I managed to calm him down and invited him to my meeting with Max the following day.

We all sat down with Max; his face was like that of an angel. It was impossible to fathom that that angelic face could speak a nasty word to a woman. In fact, he was so shy that his only way of communicating with the other sex was through violence. We explained to him that if he ever spoke in a violent manner to any of the girls in the house or to my cleaner, he would be removed from the house without notice. I also gave him his notice of non-renewal of contract that day.

A few days later, Max called me to inform me that he had some wood bugs in his room. I thought that was strange because we never had any problem like that with the house before. I went to his room and checked everything, but I didn't find anything. Still, I spread anti-woodlice powder around the inside and outside of his room and left him the remaining bottle to use if he ever saw one again. I noted that his room was full of vegetables and fresh food and advised him to store them in the kitchen instead of his room. He had several boxes of the stuff. After a few days, he called again to say that there were slugs in his room. I told him to remove all the fresh food in his room and clean the area. He could not quite understand the link between the bugs in his room and lettuce.

When his departure date arrived, he moved out quietly, never to be heard from again.

Mike

I never thought I would fall for a tenant's scam. I thought I had more or less seen it all. Mike proved me wrong. He was a very remarkable tenant who paid his rent on time and never complained about anything. He was in one of my houses for just four months, working as an engineering intern in Bristol.

A week before he left the house, he asked me whether I would buy a chest of drawers he bought from Ikea for £45. I told him that I did not need any more furniture for the room. He insisted, though because he did not want to carry it all the way back to Belgium. I asked how much he wanted for it, and he responded, 'Forty pounds.' I told him, 'I'll only take it for twenty pounds.' He asked, 'How about twenty-five pounds?' I replied, 'Twenty pounds, take it or leave it.' He agreed on that price. When he left the room, I performed the exit inventory to make sure that the furniture was left behind. Everything was fine. I returned the deposit after ten days, as I agreed to do.

When the new tenant moved into that room, I noticed that, in his entry inventory form, the chest of drawers was not listed. I asked about it, and he responded that there was no drawer when he moved in. I immediately guessed that a tenant of the house had gone into the room and taken it. I texted all the tenants straight away: 'If you took the chest's drawer, please return it.' I didn't receive a single reply. I sent a second text, but again heard nothing back. Therefore, I decided to call them one by one. The first person I called was the one who took it. I asked her why, and she told me that Mike, the seller, had sold it to her for £20. Now that was a riddle!

I sent an e-mail to Mike, asking him for an explanation. He denied selling it to the other person but acknowledged selling it to me. I had a proof of sale, his work address, and his home address; he knew I could cause some damage. I asked the girl to e-mail him about the purchase of the drawer and copy me. Finally, he agreed that he had sold it to her the day he left with the thought that I would not honour my word. I asked him to reimburse the girl if he wanted to avoid any trouble. He did so immediately. The whole situation was really weird. He was not a bad person, just someone who thought he could get away with a trick.

Joesh

If you are eating something right now, I would advise you to skip this paragraph and come back to it later. This one is very ugly.

Joesh was one of my tenants, and he was really into heavy metal music. He had long hair and always wore a black T-shirt. He was very quiet and only ever ate microwave dinners. Further, he never bothered me for anything and always paid on time. He was the ideal tenant, some might say.

Indeed, he was the ideal tenant until one evening when he came back home totally drunk. At seven o'clock in the morning, I received a call from one of the other tenants who informed me that Joesh had sprayed the downstairs toilet with shit. I asked my tenant to explain the word *shit*. 'Was it vomit or something else?' I asked. He screamed into the phone, 'Shit! Everywhere!' I did not want to see the situation in person, so I told the guy to put a note on the toilet door asking him to clean his mess. I also asked him to knock on Joesh's door to make sure he was okay. A few hours later, the same tenant called me to explain that Joesh had cleaned up his mess and apologised for his inexplicable behaviour.

The next time I saw Joesh, we avoided talking about the incident. He was a remarkable tenant thereafter. The tenant who called me initially told me one day that he often pondered how Joesh managed to get his dung on the ceiling. I'll leave that to your imagination.

Daniel

Daniel was introduced to me by the council. I remember someone from the Bristol city council calling to ask whether I would take a young, part-time professional as a tenant. That was at the beginning of my journey; I remember being quite relieved that the council was sending business my way. The gentleman first came to see the property and make sure that it was compliant with their criteria. Within a couple of days, he came back and booked an appointment for Daniel to introduce himself. When the day came, Daniel did not show up. We rebooked the appointment for another day, though, and Daniel turned up that time. He was a tall, slim, twenty-four-year-old man, the type who could be a model or a gigolo if he was in his right mind. The room he was taking was £310. The council agreed to pay £269, leaving just £41 for his share. Even though he was only working part-time, I didn't suspect that amount would cause any problems. I was totally wrong.

Within a month, Daniel managed to lose his job as a photographer at a zoo. I asked him whether there would be any problem paying his top-up fee, but he assured me that it wouldn't be an issue. I decided to wait and see. After two months, I noticed that his first top-up had not arrived . . . or the second. Thus, I decided to call the council. They again assured me that they would get in touch with him and get the situation sorted. I left the matter for about a week. After another week passed with no payments, I paid him a visit at the house. It was eleven o'clock in the morning, and he was drunk out of his mind. There were bottles of cheap cider all over the place, so I asked another tenant who was responsible for the mess. He told me that all the bottles belonged to Daniel. He also told me that he was not only jobless but also a depressed drunkard. He told me that he got fired from his job because he always turned up late. I tried to speak with him, but he was so out of his face that I decided to leave him alone for the time being.

I called the council to tell them that I needed him out of my house. He was not only refusing to pay his top-up rent, but he was damaging the house with his reckless behaviour. I told them that his presence was affecting the paying tenants living in the house. The council answered, 'You have a six-month contract with him. You cannot kick him out. You will need to take him to court.' I could not believe what I heard. At the time, I did not know that one had to take a bad tenant to court to get him or her out of the house. I regained my senses and asked the council about the procedure required to kick someone out. They were quite helpful, I have to say. Unfortunately, I could not do anything until the six-month term was over. I finally managed to get him out after eight months, but I never understood why a young, able-bodied man would choose to waste his life in such a way. I later learned that he had fathered quite a few children here and there and could not handle his good looks. Someone please pinch me! Or should I feel sorry for him?

Ismael

One of my tenants, Ismael, sent me an e-mail informing me that three bags of food were accidentally delivered to their house on a Saturday afternoon. The bags were left in front of the entrance door. Two days later, they were still there. Ismael sent me the following message:

Hello,

Maybe you are tired of me because I am always asking things. Sorry about that. This time, I would like to ask if you know something about the three bags full of food (apparently from someone who was moving from house to house) that ended up at our main door last Friday, 18/01/13. If you know something, please let us know.

My reply to him was simple: 'Eat it!'

Ale

This person entered one of my houses immediately after the previous tenant left. I remember he was in a hurry to get a place. I did not meet him personally, because he came through one of my assistants. I only met him about a month after he had moved in. I first encountered him when I was doing my monthly house inspections to ensure that the house was being maintained well. When I walked into the house, the first smell was that of tobacco. I prohibit smoking in all my houses, and it's hard to miss the signs around the house.

I knocked on Ale's door. I knew he was the one smoking because his room was near the entrance where it smelled strongest and the smell was a new to the house. Plus, I knew no other tenants smoked.

I knocked on his door and asked him whether he was smoking in the house. He defensively shouted, 'No!' I thought to myself, *Taiwo, this guy thinks you are dumb as a donkey!* I asked him again, 'Are you smoking in your room?' Again, he yelled, 'No!' I kindly reminded him that smoking was not permitted in the house, which included his room. I told him to step outside and enjoy his cigarettes in the garden. I thought that would be the end of it. Wrong!

Two weeks later, I decided to make an unexpected visit to the house. When I walked in, I could tell that Ale was still smoking in his room. When I knocked on his door, a cloud of smoke escaped from his room and into my face. I stated, 'Ale, you know this is a no smoking house.' He replied, 'I'm not smoking; it's incense! I said, 'Incense that smells like tobacco?!' Looking deep into my eyes, he finally shouted, 'Yes!' I did not know what to do. I thought, *This guy is either high or a daredevil.* And then I remembered what my handyman once told me: 'Whenever tenants open their mouths, it's to tell a lie.' He seemed to be right.

I decided to reiterate the rules and regulations of the country, thinking that things might be different in his native country. It took twenty minutes to explain my policies. And then I left, proud that I did not lose my temper. I was feeling good; no one could get to me.

Two weeks later, I decided to pop in again. Guess what? Do I need to paint the picture? Smoke! The house and carpet were infused with the odour of stale tobacco. Ale worked night shifts, so I was confident he would be home. When I knocked on his door, he opened it, clearly not very happy to see me. I said, 'You are smoking again.' He finally admitted to the offence and said, 'I smoke in my room. I pay for the room; I can do anything I want in it.' I told him flatly that he could *not* smoke in the room. The argument went on for another ten minutes. Eventually, he conceded and told me he would only smoke outdoors.

Did I win? Not at all! About a month later, my cleaner started complaining about the house. She claimed that Ale was still smoking in the house and that I should do something about it. I decided to pay him another visit. That time, he insisted that he was not the only one smoking in the house, that the other tenants smoked as much as he did. I asked him for the names of the people he had seen smoking in the house, but he responded, 'I will not tell on them.' I said, 'I can only rely on what I have seen. And you're the only person I have seen smoking in the house.' I gave him an ultimatum: 'If I smell any more smoke in the house (including your room), I will give you a notice to quit.'

Just before Christmas, one of the good tenants decided to leave because Ale was still smoking. When the holidays rolled around, he was back in his country and the house smelled like roses. During that period, my staff was away, so I had to cover most of the viewings. During my visits to the house, it smelled fresh and clean. I figured he had finally adopted my rules. One evening, I had a viewing at the house and was welcomed by a cloud of smoke. I thought to myself, *The troublemaker is back!*

As I was doing my viewing, the potential tenant said that he was not looking for a house that allowed smoking. I told him that it was a non-smoking house, but one of the tenants did not follow the rules. There and then, I knocked on his door. When he came out, he told me immediately that he was not smoking. The guy I was showing the room to busted out laughing. Until then, I thought I was dreaming. I was very angry and relieved at the same time, so I just decided to join him in laughter. I decide not to waste my time and told Ale that he would be receiving an eviction letter the following day.

I dropped off the letter indicating that he had four weeks to leave. He said he would not leave, that I would have to take him to court. I said I would take him to court and ask for compensation for the time wasted, the court fees, and the requisite change of locks. In short, he would lose his deposit and pay a lot more. I told him that I would not ask for anything less than £5,000 from the court. He packed his bags and was gone within two weeks.

Hayden

Hayden stayed in one of my houses for a period of six months. He was a very charming man—a well-paid engineer—but he was not the cleanest person I had ever met. He asked me after a couple of months of being in the house whether his girlfriend could join him. I said I had no problem with that as long as the other tenants did not moan about it. He told me that he had spoken with them and they were amenable to the idea. Out of curiosity, I asked him where she came from. He told me she was from Australia and had been travelling the world for the past year. I soon met his girlfriend. She was very friendly and called me whenever I had a letter waiting at the house. She also sent back all mail that had erroneously ended up at the house. The house was a boy's house, so having a female was pretty awesome.

After five months, I received an urgent end-of-tenancy letter from Hayden. He gave me his one month's notice, so I was happy to oblige. I thought nothing of it and sent him the waiver form so he could get his deposit back on time. When he left the house, I got calls from other tenants telling me that they had been getting bedbug bites for some time. I thought to myself, *The house was newly refurbished and all the furniture, including the beds and mattresses, were all brand new. How could there be bedbugs in the house?* I decided to do an Internet search to find out a bit more. I read that bedbugs had been putting a great strain on many hotels that had 'contracted' the pests due to the amount of travellers coming and going. I also read that it was not really a hygiene issue; some of the cleanest hotels had bedbugs. Basically, some travellers carried them in their luggage and spread them to other places. After reading that fact, I called an exterminator who was kind enough to come the following day. He inspected the house and found that Hayden's room and bed were full of bugs; the adjacent rooms were just starting to get them.

I asked the exterminator to work on all rooms, furniture, walls, and beds in the house. He told me that the size of the eggs and the bugs indicated that they had been introduced into the house around six months ago, if not earlier. It seemed clear that Hayden's girlfriend was the source of the problem.

When I passed that information onto to him, he was furious. He told me that the reason he left so suddenly was because of the bugs. I asked him why he never reported it, and he said that he did not want me to think that it was him who introduced it into the house. I then told him that he wasn't responsible, his girlfriend was. I told him that his deposit would go towards the cleaning of the entire house. He was not very happy about that fact, but that was the only thing I could do.

Gonzal

I often get calls from tenants concerning the management of their gas box. Whenever I change a gas meter into a pay-as-you-go model, I always leave the guide on the fridge or at the house's entrance. It is the responsibility of the tenants to read it.

This gentleman, Gonzal, had been in the house for four months, so I assumed he was familiar with the way things worked around the house. I was completely wrong. I got a call from him one evening because the boiler was broken. I knew the real problem had something to do with the settings of the gas box or the pressure valves. I asked him to check the pressure, and he said it was fine; I asked whether there was credit on the gas box, and he told me there was a £30 credit. Finally, I asked whether he had turned on the gas box. He told me he had because that was not the first time he topped-up the gas. But because I was not near the house (and because he had run through all my checks), I decided to inform the agency. They immediately sent someone out into the wintry weather. The gas man came and left within five minutes. He said that they had run out of gas and passed that information to the agency. And they proceeded to tell me off. I was billed £60 for the unnecessary call out, but I just passed it on to the whole house. They all moaned about it. I told them the decision was final and advised that they read the gas box instructions again.

Diego

I met Diego through a former tenant of mine. He had a budget of £450 per month for a large room. I usually did not consider anyone above thirty-five because, beyond that line, people tended to be settled in their lifestyle and not suitable for house sharing. I have had many viewings in which older people walked out immediately because the place did not live up to their high expectations. Times have changed, and most folks from older generations are not aware of the market.

Anyway, Diego arrived in the country with a job lined up, so I decided to go outside the book and take him on. The first month was fine, but then came the second month. It was apparent to me that he was struggling to come up with his rent. Fortunately, experience taught me to identify financial struggle before it got out of hand. I'm always cautious in the following situations: when tenants cannot pay the full deposit or full rent from the start; when they don't pay their second month's rent on time; when they refuse to pick up my calls or text reminders; when I see them at home too often during business hours (unless they work night shifts).

Diego exhibited all those warning signs. I immediately called him for a meeting in my office. I knew that he was old enough to be my father, so I simply suggested that he should consider moving into a much cheaper and smaller room. I also asked him whether he really needed all that space for himself. I explained that the room would be more suitable for a couple instead of one person. Further, I indicated that it would be helpful to have the room back by the end of the month because I had a couple willing to take it. I proposed that he could move into a £350 standard double room without losing his deposit or having to search for a replacement tenant. I made him believe that he was helping me out instead of insinuating that he was struggling. He found my suggestion very helpful and agreed to downgrade his room. We both felt happy about the decision. I got my room back, which I rented out the following day, and he felt more comfortable in a cheaper room. Plus, he didn't have to give up his gentlemanly pride.

In most cases, my tenants are good, honest people. Their attitudes change, however, when they lose their jobs or break up with their girlfriends. As you may have guessed, most of my tenants are male. I have often asked myself, *Where are all the women?* But then I take a look at the people around me. The ones who have bought and settled down quickly after their studies are female. Most of my female partners have boyfriends living with them in the home they bought themselves. I believe it can be chalked up to a fear of commitment, mainly. Women seem to grow up more quickly and build their nests earlier than most men. In many cases, when a relationship falls apart, the woman gets to keep the house while the man walks away. It is a sad reality.

Maxime

Maxime sent the following e-mail to me:

Hello,

I am writing to inform you about the current problems in my room and the house, but I'm sure you are already aware of them. There are many serious issues that are still not fixed despite a very long wait:

1. There are many white things on the walls in my room, which I believe is mould. The paint from the ceiling is also falling off. As a matter of fact, while I was asleep, some small bits and pieces fell on my face one night. I moved the bed a few inches away from the walls. I have started feeling unwell because of this mould issue. This is a serious health issue, and I will be checking it with the local council.
2. As far as I've been informed, some of the previous tenants still have the keys. This is a huge security issue for me. Also, there have been times when visitors came to the house without us being informed.

3. I rented this place because the advertisement claimed there was a weekly cleaner. I only saw someone 'cleaning' two or three times in two months. The only thing she didn't really do was clean.
4. Why is there only one garbage bin? Where is the other one? There are four people living in the house now.

All these issues are very serious. Technically, you are breaching the HMO landlord—tenant obligations regarding disrepair. You are also causing health hazards.

I am sure *you* would never live in such a place. I will be expecting immediate action to sort out these issues or I will move out at once and claim my deposit and the rent I've already paid.

Thanks,

Maxime

I responded to him in short order:

Hi,

Regarding the mould, it is your responsibility to ventilate your room. Mould only grows when there is too much condensation. You can get rid of it by cleaning it with bleach. Please dry your clothes in the washer dryer or in the communal area rather than in your room.

Regarding previous tenants. Why do you believe they still have keys? Have you seen anyone coming in? We are doing a lot of maintenance in the houses, but we always inform you beforehand. We also have an empty room to fill, so we do viewings.

The cleaner comes weekly. This is more than many landlords offer. It is up to all of you to top-up the cleaning. As far as I know, no one in the house does anything to maintain the cleanliness of the place. We cannot do more than that without having to increase your rent.

If you feel that your garbage bin is insufficient, please feel free to request more from the city council. There should be a black wheelie bin, a black recycle bin, a green recycle bin, and a brown food waste bin at the house. Observe the recycling rules and there will be sufficient room for your garbage.

Regarding HMO regulations, although we apply the rules, that type of house (two floors) does not require a licence.

Kind regards,

Taiwo

This tenant gave me his notice two days after my response. And he left the house three days after that. What I later learned was that the house was far from his place of work. Instead of explaining his situation to me, however, he thought it was better to find faults with the house. This happens all the time: tenants who want to break their contracts will always try to blame the house. I can't believe they think their stories are plausible.

Alex

This tenant sent me the following e-mail:

Hi,

The TV has not worked since I moved in. Can you solve the problem, please?

Best regards,

Alex

I responded to him promptly with the following message:

Hi, Alex:

It does work. Have you asked the other tenants?

Some tenants find it normal to ask me how the house is managed by the existing tenants. This is a classic example of poor communication. The tenant had been living in the house for a few days, but he did not think to ask his housemates how the TV worked; instead, he found the time and energy to e-mail me with a request to show him myself. After receiving my e-mail, though, I never heard from him again.

Another classic example is when a tenant loses his entrance key. He or she often asks me to open the door instead of getting in touch with the other tenants.

Tip: remember that tenants pay for the following things:

- **The loss of their keys—if I am not around to open the door for them, they will have to call a locksmith and sort themselves out**
- **The blocked drains in the toilet and bathroom**
- **The cost of removing any unwanted items left in the house**
- **The cost of getting rid of vermin due to poor hygiene in the house**

SOME LEGAL THINGS YOU SHOULD KNOW

This final chapter will take us back to what spurred our interest in this field: the dream of becoming (professional) landlords. As landlords, we can be emotionally attached to our investments.

I have to accept the fact that I have reacted emotionally to situations in the past due to my lack of knowledge. Eventually, I was led to study the law surrounding the industry, and it is my duty as a Rent2Rent coach to share all my findings with you.

What you will read here is just a snapshot of what you ought to know. Please consult your solicitor whenever necessary. These rules are not only for landlords, but also for Rent2Rent managers. Having this knowledge will empower you to request specific things from your agents and landlords. And most importantly, it will help you handle your tenants correctly. Please note that the rules are constantly changing, so please keep yourselves updated on the latest regulations.

Here are some things you should know whilst building your Rent2Rent business:

- Estate agents are governed by a number of laws. Letting and management agents adhere to fewer government laws; instead, they are governed mostly by common laws
- The common law is interested in protecting the client, the landlord. It is silent about any duties owed to tenants
- A lease is a tenancy, a contract between you and the tenant

A lease will exist if:

- The lease or tenancy agreement grants the tenant exclusive possession
- Rent is charged
- The lease/tenancy exists for a stated period of time

A lease can last anywhere between 1 week and 999 years. A licence to occupy does not grant the licensee/lodger the exclusive possession of the house; it is different from a lease/tenancy. In short, the lodger will be a licensee, not a tenant. A licensee might still pay rent and occupy the space for a certain period of time, but he or she does not automatically have the right to exclude others from living at the property as a tenant would. Essentially, a licensee does not enjoy the same rights as a tenant.

Any tenancy or agreement between you and the landlord that exceeds three years becomes a deed. This stipulation includes residential tenancies. This designation is a requirement under the Law of Property Act 1925, section 52. Previously, deeds had to be signed, sealed, and delivered to be valid, but the Law of Property (Miscellaneous Provisions) Act 1989 abolished that rule. Rather, a deed must be described as such, signed in the presence of a witness, and delivered as a deed. So if you intend to take contracts beyond three years, you must do so via a deed. Tenancies that last for a shorter period of time than three years can be arranged orally. Always use the words *subject to contract,* though to avoid any legally binding blunders.

Each tenant named on the contract is fully responsible for the payment of the full rent and any repairs. Each tenant is jointly and severally liable.

Covenants are promises made by one party to another. Leases contain covenants that involve promises made by the tenant to the landlord (commonly) and the landlord to the tenant (infrequently). One of the covenants extending from the landlord to the tenants is the promise of quiet enjoyment of the property.

Housing Act 1988 Tenancies

The Housing Act 1988 revolutionised residential lettings in the private sector by introducing assured tenancies and assured shorthold tenancies. Without this act, Rent2Rent would not be possible; without this act, the buy-to-let boom would not have happened.

The Housing Act 1988 came into effect on 15 January 1989. It was introduced because the government wanted to strengthen the private sector market by creating tenancies that gave landlords more freedom to choose their tenants. This freedom was expanded even further through the amendments introduced in 1996.

Before this act, landlords could not seek possession of their properties freely. Contracts were protected. Before 1988, all tenancies were automatically assured tenancies. ASTs had to be created by serving a prescribed notice under section 20 of the act. If served incorrectly, the contract was an assured tenancy. Although this act introduced some freedom to the landlords, it was nevertheless tricky. A small mistake could turn an AST into an assured tenancy. Therefore, for an AST to exist, a section 20 notice had to be served on the tenant before the start of the tenancy. This complication was eased by the Housing Act of 1996, which was more friendly towards landlords and granted them more freedom. The act came into force on 28 February 1997 to amend the Housing Act 1988.

The amendments are as follows:

- Tenancies after 28 February 1997 are automatically ASTs, not assured tenancies
- The section 20 notice is no longer needed to create an AST
- To create an assured tenancy, the tenant must be advised in writing before the start; no formal notice is needed
- The tenancy must state that the tenancy being entered into is not an AST. Failure to do so, however, will not create an assured tenancy
- ASTs can last for fewer than six months

Assured Tenancy	Assured Shorthold Tenancy
• More protection of tenants if landlords request possession • Landlords must prove grounds for possession • Tenants have the right to stay for as long as they want • Landlords must serve a section 8 notice • Fixed period or indefinite and periodic • Tenancy must last for a minimum of six months	• Created automatically • Limited security of tenure for the tenants • Landlords can seek repossession using a section 8 notice or a section 21 notice without any reasoning • Periodic and fixed-term tenancies • Tenancy can last for any period of time

Assured tenancy and AST can only be created if the following conditions are met:

- The tenant is an individual, not a company, charity, or trust
- The property is the tenant's main home
- The landlord is not a resident
- The rent does not exceed £100,000 per year

Acts of Parliament and statutory regulations do not govern tenancies; the common law and contract law do provide some structure, however. If a tenancy is not a Housing Act 1988 tenancy, some sort of agreement is needed to make it viable. These agreements are known as non-housing act tenancy agreements. The following are examples of these sorts of agreements:

- Law of contract agreement (LOC)
- Company lets (leases)
- Holiday lets
- Common law tenancies

These agreements are created outside the Housing Act and count as contracts. Thus, none of the provisions of the Housing Act 1988 apply to them. You cannot serve a section 21 notice to end a tenancy in these agreements.

Eviction for Non Housing Act 1988 Tenancies

Under the common law, for non Housing Act 1988 tenancies, possession of property can be established in two different ways:

- When the fixed term finishes (effluxion of time); the contract ends on the final day automatically
- When it is renewed periodically and automatically (unless a notice to quit is served—usually after four weeks' notice is given)

Notice to quit is usually related to the period of the lease. Weekly tenancies require a week's notice; monthly tenancies require a month's notice; quarterly tenancies require a quarter of a year's notice; tenancies one year long or longer require six months' notice.

The Protection from Eviction Act 1977 overrides the common law rules and insists that any notice to quit must be in writing and given with at least four weeks' notice. However, if the notice period in the lease is longer, the lease details supersede the 1977 act. Remember: four weeks is the *minimum* notice that must be given.

The notice to quit must contain prescribed information. The list can be found in Notice to Quit Regulations 1988. The notice to quit must explain the following terms:

- The landlord must gain a possession order from the court before evicting the tenant
- Application for the possession order cannot be made until the notice period of the notice to quit has expired
- The receiver of the notice must be told he or she can get advice from a solicitor, citizens' advice bureau, or any other housing aid associations

It is a criminal offence to try to gain possession without a court order. Again, the Protection Eviction Act 1977 requires a minimum of four weeks' notice in writing.

Evictions for Assured Tenancies

In your Rent2Rent business, you will probably never deal with an assured tenancy eviction unless you decide to employ this strategy with retirement homes that bestow a high level of tenancy security on your tenants. I am including this section because one of my former students is looking to expand into this lucrative market. When using assured tenancies, one must be aware that tenants cannot be forced to move easily. Unless some critical grounds can be demonstrated, it can be very difficult to get the property back.

There are two grounds for possession:

- Mandatory grounds
- Discretionary grounds

This table provides more information:

Mandatory Grounds

Grounds	Explanation	Prior Notice Needed	Notice Period to Activate
1	The landlord occupied the premises at some time as an only or principal home, gave notice of possible intention to return, and decides to do so.	Yes	Two months
2	A mortgagee of the property wishes to obtain possession to exercise a power of sale and sell with vacant possession. The mortgage must exist at the start of the tenancy.	Yes	Two months
3	Premises, within the last twelve months, have been the subject of a holiday letting. They must be let for a fixed term of up to eight months, and the notice of need for renewed holiday letting must be given.	Yes	Two weeks

4	The premises belong to an educational institution that normally lets the spaces to students, and the spaces have been let in that manner within the last twelve months.	Yes	Two weeks
5	The premises were let to a minister of religion and are currently required for another minister.	Yes	Two months
6	The landlord intends to demolish or reconstruct the whole dwelling (or a substantial part of the dwelling). Alternatively, the landlord intends to carry out substantial work on the dwelling or part of the dwelling and cannot complete the work without the tenant giving up his or her possession.	No	Two months
	NB: the landlord cannot use this ground if the tenancy existed before the landlord bought the premises or the tenancy follows from a Rent Act 1977 tenancy. If the landlord is successful and regains possession, he or she must pay the tenant's reasonable removal costs (Housing Act 1988, section 11).	No	Two months
7	The tenancy is a periodic tenancy that has devolved under the will or intestacy of the former tenant and proceedings are initiated within twelve months of death (or the date the landlord received notice of the death), even if he or she has continued to accepted rent. NB: this ground cannot be used against a legal transmission—a transfer as a gift to a surviving spouse or a relative for tax reasons (Housing Act 1988, section 17).	No	Two weeks

8	Rent arrears are owed exceeding eight weeks' (for weekly tenants) or two months' (for monthly tenants) rent; or for quarterly tenants, at least three months' rent is in arrears; or for yearly tenants, at least three months' rent is three months in arrears. The arrears need to exist at the date of service of the notice *and* at the date of the hearing.

Discretionary grounds

Grounds	Explanation	Prior Notice Needed	Notice Period to Activate
9	Suitable alternative accommodations are available for the tenant or will be available when the order for possession takes effect.	No	Two months
10	Some rent is lawfully due from the tenant and is in arrears. NB: the amounts do not have to meet the limits in ground 8.	No	Two weeks
11	The tenant has persistently delayed paying rent that is lawfully due. NB: there do not have to be any arrears.	No	Two weeks
12	There has been a breach of covenant by the tenant.	No	Two weeks
13	The condition of the property or common parts has deteriorated because of waste (damage) committed by the tenant or those for whom he or she is responsible.	No	Two weeks

14	The ground was extended by section 148 of the Housing Act 1996. This applies when a tenant, sub-tenant, lodger, or visitor meets the following criteria: Has been found guilty of conduct causing or likely to cause an annoyance to a person residing, visiting, or otherwise engaging in a lawful activity in the locality. Has been convicted of using the premises or allowing it to be used for illegal or immoral purposes; or has committed an arrestable offence in or in the locality of the property.	No	Date of service of the notice; no notice period required
14A	(This ground was inserted by section 149 of the Housing Act 1996.) The landlord is a registered social landlord or charitable housing trust and allows recovery when one partner has left due to domestic violence and the court is satisfied that the victim is unlikely to return. The landlord must have served (or made an effort to serve) notice to the party who has left.	No	Two weeks
15	The condition of any furniture provided by the landlord has deteriorated because of misuse by the tenant, sub-tenant, or lodger.		
16	The tenancy was a service tenancy, and the tenant left employment.	No	Two months
17	(This was inserted by section 102 of the Housing Act 1996.) The tenant induced the landlord to grant the tenancy by knowingly or recklessly making a false statement.	No	Two weeks

If a mandatory ground is proven, the court must grant possession. If a discretionary ground is proven, the court will not necessarily grant possession—it will grant possession only if it deems that action just and reasonable. The court might warn the tenant not to breach the contract again. And if the tenant does breach the contract once more, the court will be more likely to award possession. In this context, notice must be served to the tenant at the start of the contract. The notice must state that, if any breach is made, the landlord might rely on the grounds to seek possession of the property.

Different grounds need different notice periods. The time period ranges from two weeks to two months.

Evictions for Assured Shorthold Tenancies

Section 21

The eviction notice must be in writing. You can obtain a copy from your local council. There are two types of section 21 evictions, depending upon when the notice was served. Both require a two-month notice and are differentiated here:

- Service within the fixed term. The notice cannot expire before the end of the fixed term
- Service during the periodic term. It must be in line with the periodic term; i.e., weekly or monthly periodic terms must include a two-month notice period. Similarly, quarterly terms must have quarterly notice periods and yearly terms must have six-month notice periods. The notice must expire on the last day of the period

You can only serve section 21 eviction notices after the first six months of a contract has elapsed. You do not need to give any reason for seeking possession of the property. You can get standard forms from your local housing department; otherwise, I have listed some key elements for your consideration here. Your notice must adhere to the following standards:

- It must be in writing
- You must warn the tenant that a court order is needed to enforce the possession
- You must give at least two months' notice
- You must have protected his or her deposit with a government scheme

Tenants with assured tenancies have a high level of protection. If a landlord wants to gain possession, he or she must serve a section 8 notice and prove one or more grounds for possession, as laid out in the Housing Act 1988, section 2. Landlords using ASTs can use either section 8 or section 21.

The fastest way to evict a tenant—a procedure that I have used three times myself—is the accelerated possession procedure. All ASTs signed since 1989 can use this fast track. Section 21 must be correctly served, and the landlord can only claim possession, not rent arrears. If you want rent arrears, you could start a small claims court at the same time. If all paperwork is in order and the tenant has no representation, the court can grant a possession order without a hearing within fourteen days.

The protection from Eviction Act 1977 was specifically introduced to prevent unlawful evictions and harassment. Please be aware that tenants or licensees can seek damages against unlawful evictions under section 27 and 28 of the act. Anyone convicted of offence can be sent to prison for anywhere between six months and two years.

There are two ways for you or the landlord to repossess a property:

- The tenant surrenders the tenancy
- You gain a court order

The tenant can also submit a notice to quit. But such a notice cannot be used by the landlord or the tenant to end a fixed period tenancy.

Health and Safety

On 1 April 2006, a new system, based on hazards, to categorise fitness for habitation was introduced. Under the new rules, the landlord is responsible for the property's structure and exterior repairs. He or she is *not* responsible for any negligence or misuse on the part of the tenants. I have a weekly cleaner who visits the houses, and I keep my eyes on my properties on a weekly basis to make sure that the space is kept in good order. I also leave my business card with neighbours so they can call me if they have any problems with my tenants.

Tenants are expected to carry out small jobs around the house. For this reason, I always post rules around the house, especially in the kitchen and bathroom.

The tenant has the right to withhold rent if the landlord refuses to carry out his repairs. Housing Health and Safety Rating System (HHSRS) is the risk assessment procedure introduced in part 1 of the Housing Act 2004 that addresses residential properties. HHSRS covers twenty-nine categories of housing hazards, as listed here:

Physiological requirements:

- Dampness and mould growth
- Excess heat
- Excess cold
- Asbestos and manufactured mineral fibres
- Biocides
- Radiation
- Uncombusted fuel gas
- Volatile organic compounds

Psychological requirements:

- Crowding and space
- Entry by intruders
- Lighting
- Noise

Protection against infection:

- Domestic hygiene, pests, and refuse
- Food safety
- Personal hygiene, sanitation, and drainage
- Water supply for domestic purposes

Protection against accidents:

- Falls associated with baths
- Falls on the level
- Falls associated with stairs and steps
- Falls between levels
- Electrical hazards
- Fire
- Hot surfaces
- Collision and entrapment
- Explosions
- Ergonomics
- Structural collapse and failing elements

Houses are rated to meet the health and safety standards if brought to the attention of the local authorities. Usually, all houses taken from an agent already meet these standards. Under the Housing Act 2004, all HMOs must meet the same health and safety standards.

What Is an HMO (Multi-Let)?

People often ask me what an HMO is. In order to fully understand the meaning, I have to provide a little background on the matter. The Housing Act 2004 (part 7, section 254) sets out the definition of a House in Multiple Occupation (HMO). The meaning is much more complex than that espoused via the previous Housing Act 1985. It tries to cover as many situations as possible. The legislation was introduced in 2006, and it required that properties be free from hazards, as defined in the Housing Act 2004. Also, properties classed as HMOs must meet the standards relating to the number of occupants; i.e., a property may be acceptable for two or three people, but it might not be suitable for four or five people.

Section 254 of the act states that a property is an HMO if it adheres to the following criteria:

- It meets the standard test
- Or it meets the self-contained flat test
- Or it meets the converted flat test
- Or an HMO licence is in force
- Or it is a converted block of flats

In this section, I will explain in more details the first three categories because they are the main three tests.

The Standard Test

A property meets a standard test and is defined as an HMO if it adheres to the following criteria:

- One or more units of living space is not a self-contained flat
- It is occupied by people who do not constitute a single household
- It is the occupier's only or main home
- The living accommodations are only used for that purpose
- At least one of the occupiers pays rent or some other form of payment
- At least two of the households in the living space share one or more basic amenities, such as a kitchen and a bathroom
- It is a converted block of flats

Two people sharing a space do not count. Three or more occupiers of two or more households are regarded HMO occupiers if the previous criteria are met.

Self-Contained Flats Test

An accommodation that features a self-contained flat is defined as an HMO if the following statements are true:

- It is occupied by people who do not form a single household
- It is the occupier's only or main home
- The living accommodation is only used for that purpose
- At least one of the occupiers pays rent or some other form of payment
- At least two of the households in the living accommodation share one or more basic amenities, such as a kitchen and a bathroom
- It is a converted block of flats

Converted Buildings Test

A building or part of it meets the converted flat test and is defined as an HMO if the following statements are true:

- It is a converted building
- It has one or more units of living space that is not a self-contained flat
- It is occupied by people who do not constitute a single household
- It is the occupier's only or main home
- The living accommodation is only used for that purpose
- At least one of the occupiers pays rent or some other form of payment

Of course, most rules have exceptions. Properties are *not* defined as HMOs if any of the following statements are true:

- It is controlled or managed by the public sector
- It is occupied by students and let by an educational establishment
- It is occupied by a religious community
- It is occupied by owners

- It is occupied by two people
- It is a single household
- It serves as the main and principal home for workers

HMOs or multi-lets can be any type of house or bungalow up to two storeys tall. The HHSRS must be met, but you do not need a licence even though the property is classified as an HMO. Some HMO properties, as stipulated by the provisions of the Housing Act 2004, mandate a licence.

In addition, you must consider selective licensing, which gives the local authority the power to decide that a property must be licensed. This can happen if the local authority is not happy with the way a property is being managed or the property encompasses an entire postal code region. This often occurs in areas marked out for regeneration.

For a property to require a mandatory licence, all of the following criteria must be met:

- The property must be defined as an HMO, as determined by the standard test, self-contained test, and converted building test
- The property must be three or more storeys. The count includes habitable lower ground floors, attic rooms, and mezzanine floors. In addition, if a two-storey apartment is above the ground floor commercial premises, it is classified as three storeys
- The property is occupied by five or more people who form two or more households

For example, a two-storey house with five unrelated occupiers is classified as an HMO/multi-let, but it does not require a licence because it is only two storeys. Nevertheless, it must meet the HHSRS standards. Two people sharing is not an HMO; three or more occupiers of two or more households will be regarded as occupiers of an HMO.

Under the Housing Act 2004, all HMOs must meet the same health and safety standards as any other property. A contact name, address, and telephone number of the person managing the property must be clearly displayed in a prominent area of the house. HMOs with more than five occupiers must have fire notices clearly displayed.

Local authorities have the power to serve different types of notices if they suspect that the house is not being run properly. They have the power to take the following actions:

- Serve improvement notices
- Serve prohibition orders
- Serve notices to undertake emergency measures
- Serve interim or final management orders
- Serve interim or final empty dwelling management orders
- Serve overcrowding notices

The local authority will serve interim or final management orders if they think there is a risk to the health and safety of the occupiers. The local authority can also serve a notice stating the maximum occupation limit per room and the HMO if they suspect a property might be overcrowded. Appeals to a residential property tribunal are possible if you deem the judgement unfair.

For mandatory licences, the local authority will take into account whether the owner of the house is fit and proper—that is, whether he or she is in good stead with the law. The terms for application of a licence HMO is in the House Act 2004, schedule 4.

Tip: HMO licences are mandatory if the dwelling is defined as an HMO, is on three or more floors, or is occupied by five or more persons comprising two or more households.

The Safety of the Property

The Building Regulations 1991 made amendments to the Building Act 1985. It included provisions for the detection of smoke and fire in the house. Now, all new dwellings must be fitted with smoke alarms before the dwelling is completed. It must be fitted with one or more detectors and approved by the local authority. This provision also affects old dwellings that have undergone extensive renovation. The requirements are not necessary for old houses or rented property, unless they are HMOs. Rent2Rent properties are HMOs and must comply with these safety regulations. If you have battery alarms, it is the responsibility of the tenants to check and replace the batteries as needed.

Gas and Electrical Safety

The first gas safety regulations were instated in 1994. The regulations were then amended in 1998 through the Gas Regulations 1998, which came into force 31 October 1998. It placed legal duties on landlords, agents, and contractors dealing with rented properties. All gas appliances, pipework leading to the appliances, and flues from the appliances must be checked yearly. As an extra precaution, carbon monoxide detectors can be fitted in properties, but they are not currently required by law. Not complying with these regulations constitutes a criminal offence and can result in six months in prison and a £5,000 fine. In case of death, one will face a very serious charge.

Since 2009, CORGI engineers have had to re-register with Gas Safe Register. Contractors must renew their registration yearly and carry ID when they make visits. As an owner or Rent2Rent manager, you must keep records of the following things for two years:

- The property address
- The gas appliances in the property and their location
- The date of the last inspection
- Any defects identified
- Any remedial actions taken
- The name of the contractor and his or her Gas Safe registration number

The law states that current gas safety certificates must be given to tenants before they move in. Similarly, the yearly check certificates must be given to them within twenty-eight days of the inspection. Most of my Rent2Rent agents comply, but I have to chase others to get them to send in an engineer. Most of my private landlords forget about this sort of things, so I tend to send them yearly reminders and do it myself. Of course, they always pay for the engineer.

When you visit a potential Rent2Rent property and see central heating systems, stoves, or appliances using coal, oil, or wood, you might want to know their safety status, even though they are not necessitated by the regulations. There are two regulations that cover the supply of electrical equipment with a working voltage of 50-1000 volts:

- Low Voltage Electrical Equipment Regulations 1989
- Electrical Equipment (Safety) Regulations 1994

Unlike gas regulations, it is not mandatory to check electrical equipment yearly. But failing to ensure that they are safe is a criminal offence. I recommend carrying out tests at least every five years and keeping all the records.

All your electrical goods should carry the CE standard markings. If your Rent2Rent property comes fully furnished with appliances (or if you supply some electrical goods to the house, such as a microwave, kettle, or toaster), you are classified as a supplier of goods and must comply with certain safety standards. For example, the Plugs and Socket (Safety) Regulations 1994 requires all sockets and plugs to meet British standards.

In short, if you are an agent, manager, or landlord, you must have a system in place to comply with the rules. And if something goes wrong, you can use the due diligence defence in court.

Furniture Safety

I once bought furniture from the Internet without thinking about whether or not it would be suitable for my Rent2Rent business. I realised my mistake when I was giving away an old sofa bed to a charity company. The man who came to collect the bed first ensured that the compliance tag was stuck to the mattress. In the past, I have mistakenly or angrily removed those tags without thinking about it. Luckily for me, the tag on that bed was hidden somewhere, so I was able to get rid of it. After that experience, I opened the books to learn more about those regulations.

Furniture and Furnishing Regulations 1988 was amended in 1993. It applies to manufacturers, retailers, agents, and landlords. Furniture made or reupholstered after 1 March 1989 must meet the safety standards and be labelled as such. Since 1990, retailers have not been able to sell furniture that does not comply with the standard. The tag you should watch out for looks like this:

As of 1993, all furniture in rented properties must meet the given standards. Therefore, landlords and agents letting a house in the course of business must comply with the regulation. All labels must comply with British standards under the Furniture and Furnishing (Fire) (Safety) Regulations 1993. Consequently, as a Rent2Rent manager, you must comply with these rules and locate these signs when negotiating on your property. Some landlords want to leave some furniture in the house instead of storing it elsewhere, but if said furniture does not comply with the regulations, it must be removed. Fortunately, most landlords will be understanding when you explain your rationale.

Fees and Deposits

Even though there are few laws that relate specifically to residential letting and management agents and their activities, we still owe the duty of care to everyone with whom we do business. We have to operate under the following regulations:

- The Consumer Protection From Unfair Trading Regulations 2008
- The Accommodation Agencies Act 1953
- The Property Misdescriptions Act 1991
- The Cancellation of Contract Made in a Consumer's Home or Place of Work Regulations 2008

The information about your Rent2Rent accommodation cannot be misleading. Thus, your contracts must be in plain language so your potential tenant knows what he or she is getting for his or her money. If you are charging any fees (e.g., an administration fee for a credit check or a down payment fee to reserve a room), always make sure that the charges are explained thoroughly. If there are penalties in your contract, you should delineate them.

Remember: you cannot take a deposit or a fee from a potential tenant if it is not directly related to a specific property he or she plans to take. Likewise, you cannot take any payment from a potential tenant to find him or her a property. Note that, even though the latter rule is applicable to business in the United Kingdom, it is not a concern in many other countries.

Further, you cannot charge to arrange a viewing with a potential tenant. You will meet a lot of time-wasters who book viewings but don't bother to turn up. Even so, that is not a sufficient reason to charge fees. In fact, it is an offence under the Accommodation Agencies Act. Similarly, you cannot charge a potential tenant for adding him or her to your mailing list. I have many people looking for en suite rooms who give me their contact details. It would be illegal to request payment for that service. The penalty as stipulated by the Office of Fair Trading (OFT) is £3,000 or three months in prison, so it is clearly not worth the risk.

When taking fees or deposits from potential tenants, you should make sure the tenant understands what the payment is for and which property it relates to. This will prevent any confusion in the event that the potential tenant changes his or her mind. You will come across this type of situation often when advertising your rooms. When doing your viewings, always have your down payment form with you. I have created one for myself and my students, which we use when we decide to reserve a room for a client and remove it from the market. When a client signs the form, we are committing ourselves to secure him or her the accommodation; therefore, we are excluding other potential tenants from taking the room. In exchange, we require a commitment from the client, £100, which is deducted from his or her deposit when he or she signs the contract. If the client changes his or her mind, that money covers my loss. Here is an example of a down payment form:

Down Payment Form

Property address:

Date:

Amount of down payment to secure the room: £100

Name of tenant:

Tel.:

E-mail:

Anticipated date to move into the room:

PLEASE NOTE THAT YOUR DOWN PAYMENT IS NOT REFUNDABLE. BY SIGNING THIS FORM, YOU AGREE TO TAKE THE ROOM IN QUESTION AND MOVE INTO THE ROOM ON THE ANTICIPATED DATE. In return, we will hold the room for you and withdraw all further advertisements and viewings of this room.

IF YOU WITHDRAW FOR ANY REASON, WE WILL NOT REFUND YOU THE DOWN PAYMENT.

Signature:

Date:

Name:

Tip: although there are few regulations that specifically govern the residential and management industry, it is implied that we all abide by the code of practice set up by professional bodies such as ARLA and NLA.

Protecting Your Deposits

The Housing Act 2004 also introduced the Tenancy Deposit Schemes for ASTs. All deposits must be registered within thirty days of receipt and returned to tenants within ten days of departure. If the deposit is not registered, the landlord, agent, or manager cannot serve a section 21 notice, and he or she can be fined three times the deposit.

There are three different agencies you can use:

- TDS: The Tenancy Deposit Scheme
- TDSL: The Tenancy Deposit Solutions Ltd
- DPS: The Deposit Protection Service

Deposits can be insured or custodial. If a deposit is custodial, once the tenant pays the deposit, the money is transferred to the scheme within thirty days. If there is a dispute at the end of the end of tenancy agreement, the scheme holds the deposit until the dispute is resolved. If a deposit is insured, once the tenant pays the deposit, the landlord, agent, or manager must transfer the money into the client's account. The client account must be opened with your bank. A small premium is paid to insure this deposit, usually £15-£30 per protected deposit.

In both cases, the tenant must be given information about the way his or her deposit is being protected and ways to seek advice in case of a dispute. This section of the law has been revised quite a bit over the last few years, so please keep yourselves well informed. Most Rent2Rent managers have to protect their deposits under the custodial setting unless they are a member of a property body.

Implied Obligations

As an agent, you must always give some form of notice before entering your tenants' rooms. It is implied that you must allow the tenant quiet enjoyment of the rooms. In general, there are fewer obligations for landlords than for tenants. Tenants are expected to act in a 'tenant-like manner.' This means that they are expected to carry out some small jobs in the house, such as cleaning the sinks, changing light bulbs, and testing smoke alarms regularly. Be forewarned that many tenants will illogically expect *you* to carry out those duties for them.

Additional Clauses

If you are using a letting agent to obtain your Rent2Rent properties, it is important to be aware of the type of contract you're signing. All contracts are open to negotiations; clauses can be added or removed. Any clause that you do not feel comfortable with should be addressed before you sign. You must be aware of the content and implications of any additional clauses, especially the break clauses.

You may add an option to renew if you sense that you might want to keep the property for at least three years. I often do this if I invest in upgrading a property. After all, I do not want the landlord to put the house on the market after I have invested some money in it. The option to renew is entirely yours, not the landlord's. The landlord does not have the option to refuse if you wish to exercise this option. Also, the option to renew outweighs a break clause. For example, if your tenancy lasts for one year with additional clauses to renew for two more years, you can keep the house for three years if you wish. You can also opt not to renew it.

Housing Benefits

The Local Housing Allowance was introduced on 7 April 2008. A housing benefit is also known as a rent rebate or a rent allowance. It is a government scheme paid by local authorities, and it is designed to help out low-income tenants. The rate depends upon the size of the property and family as well as the claimant's income, savings, and age. The entitlement is currently capped at the rate of a four-bedroom house or £400, whichever is lower. Please liaise with your local council to learn about any changes. You can apply to have the rent paid directly to you under the following circumstances:

- The tenant is considered vulnerable and wishes to have the payment issued directly to you
- The tenant is in arrears of eight weeks or more
- The local authority believes it will help secure a tenancy
- The rent is reduced to the level of the LHA for the area and size of the property

It is a criminal offence not to inform the local authorities of any overpayment or change of circumstances under the Benefit and Council Tax Benefit Amendment Regulations 1997. Any overpayment can be claimed up to six years after the overpayment under the Social Security Administration Act 1997.

The Housing Benefit Regulations 1997 allow local authorities to demand information from anyone receiving housing benefits. It is a criminal offence not to respond to a local authority's demand for information relating to a housing benefit tenancy. You have up to four weeks to respond to any request. Failure to do so might result in a £1,000 fine and £40 per day until the information is provided.

When to Use a Deed instead of an AST

Under the Law Of Property Act 1952, section 52, any land-related transaction (including residential tenancies) lasting longer than three years must be created by a deed. For Rent2Rent managers, when dealing with a landlord who agrees to a long-term deal, you need to have a deed contract in place rather than an AST. It must be clearly written on the document that the agreement is intended to be a deed.

The requirements of a deed are as follows:

- The document must be signed in the presence of a witness who confirms the signature
- The document must be delivered as a deed by the signatory or someone authorised by him or her to do so on his or her behalf
- The document must be in writing

Tip: oral contracts can be binding. When dealing with tenants or landlords, you can have an oral agreement, but always use the words *subject to contract* on any correspondence. Oral contracts are as valid as written ones.

List of useful online resources:

- www.hse.gov.uk

- www.legislation.gov.uk

- www.naea.co.uk

- www.rics.org

- www.arla.co.uk

- www.communities.gov.uk

- www.gassaferegister.co.uk

- www.hmrc.gov.uk

- www.niceic.org.uk

- www.mydeposits.co.uk

- www.depositprotection.com

- www.thedisputeservice.co.uk

- www.tpos.co.uk

- www.tds.gb.com

SOME ARTICLES

I regularly contribute to some magazines and newspapers. Here are some of the articles I have submitted most recently:

What Is Rent2Rent™?

Rent2Rent™ means taking control of a property from a struggling landlord and transforming it into a corporate/Multi-let accommodation instead. Depending on your target market, an upgrade of the property might be needed. This might range from a simple coat of paint to installing a new bathroom.

Rent2Rent™ is not a lease option; you do not buy or promise to buy the property after a number of years. You simply rent the property from either a letting agent or a private landlord on a long-term contract with the permission to upgrade it for the young professional market. Depending upon your ability to negotiate, you might pay the normal market rate or slightly less for a longer engagement period.

Rent2Rent™ requires under £4,000 to take control of a property—that is, rents, deposits, and agency fees (if applicable). You can then let out each room individually to corporate working tenants. The difference between the rent that you charge each individual tenant and the rent that you pay to the owner of the property is the **gross profit.**

You can make a minimum return on investment (ROI) of 100 per cent per year per property. In fact, the profit is quite substantial because, after letting all the rooms out to renters in the first two weeks after taking over the property, you will have made more than your initial investment.

Rent2Rent™ is the fastest way to make massive passive income in today's market. Some even say that it is the **only strategy** that makes sense in today's market. This strategy has enabled me and many of my students to increase our monthly cash flow from nothing to thousands of pounds.

I have been approached by a number of experienced landlords who find the idea of **Rent2Rent**™ blasphemous. I have also heard from a large number of landlords that they prefer this idea to the traditional way of running a property. The latter group of landlords are often based outside the United Kingdom and only concerned with eliminating voids.

Why is **Rent2Rent**™ the best strategy there is in today's property market? It is quite simple: for landlords who are seeking a secure income, renting to a **Rent2Rent**™ manager means having the rent paid, guaranteed, for the number of months or years they have agreed upon. There are no voids and they don't have to deal with many hassles. The responsibilities are well defined, and the **Rent2Rent**™ manager only calls upon the landlord when it is his or her responsibility to look into a problem.

What are the benefits for the tenant? As we all know, getting a mortgage today is an uphill battle. Having the 25 per cent deposit is not often enough; one must have a minimum income and a clean credit record. In a country that has encouraged (perhaps to the point of addiction) the use of credit cards for so long, how many candidates meet the criteria needed to get on the property ladder? Many young professionals are left in limbo, having to house share long after their student days are over.

The **Rent2Rent**™ manager manages the landlord's worries and the tenants' expectations. For this, he or she is handsomely rewarded. In short, the **Rent2Rent**™ manager does the hard work that many landlords are not prepared to do themselves; namely, managing more than one tenant per property.

I encourage anyone who wants to implement the **Rent2Rent**™ strategy to look for the right mentor first. We should never forget that there are rules and regulations to look into. For any information about my mentorship programs, please simply visit my website: www.renttorent. co.uk.

Rent2Rent™: Consent to Let

If you intend to do **Rent2Rent**™, make sure you get your consent to let.

I recently came across a person who had invested in many courses over the years but had not yet achieved great success. When he heard about **Rent2Rent**™, he decided to give it a go without looking into some basic legal issues that the strategy requires one to know. As I was getting ready to go on stage to talk, he told me that, after he secured his first **Rent2Rent**™ deal from a letting agent, the landlord decided to take a look at a property being sold nearby. The landlord decided to get a bit more nosey, actually watching the property to count who went in and out. I believe he did this for quite some time. He then approached some of the tenants to ask who they were and how many people were living in the house. When he got the facts, he realised that he could make more money and took his house back in order to sign directly with the tenants.

Unfortunately for the man I spoke to, he did not get a consent to let agreement from the landlord or agent before he started. Although the agents were fully aware of his strategy—they even found him his second deal—they still couldn't do much to help him.

It is crucial to get a written consent to let from the agent or the landlord before getting started. For this reason, I share a legal pack with my students that includes a consent to let form. The form requires the signature of the landlord or the agent if the property is fully managed by that person. This form can be added to the addendum of the contract.

You might be surprised by how much information some letting agents do not know; always take a copy of the potential contract home with you so you can read it carefully. Any clauses that make you uncomfortable should be addressed with the agent before signing. Do not get carried away by the enthusiasm that often accompanies finding a deal.

Never hide your intentions to multi-let the house from the agent because he or she will know the best landlord to suit your needs. Some landlords have specific requirements for their properties. Indeed, some landlords only want families, not sharers or students. A good agent will match you with the right landlord.

In summary, to avoid any surprises, always read your contract and get consent to let. For more information about my courses or legal materials, please visit my website: www.renttorent.co.uk.

Rent2Rent™: How and Where to Find Your Deals

Many people ask me: Why would landlords give me control of their properties, and where do I find these landlords? The first thing I explain is how I got started. If you have read my first book, **Rent2Rent: Massive Ca$h During a Massive Crash,** you know that I was once a struggling landlord who had to find a way to save my property. I found a group of young professionals who needed my house as much as I needed their cash. It worked.

'Still, why would a landlord give me control of his or her property?' you might ask. The answer depends upon personal circumstances. Some of my landlords live abroad and want to have long-term tenants in their houses. Some of them have been managing their houses for decades, but they gain a new appreciation for peace of mind. Basically, they want to rest and enjoy the income their portfolio brings them. Some of my landlords are prolific investors who buy but cannot be bothered to manage their houses. These landlords aim at capital gain. As long as they get long-term tenants who make it possible for them to pay their mortgages, they are quite contented.

The other type of landlords are those struggling to cope with their property because they accidentally inherited the house or they have been struck by streams of bad tenants. One example is a woman who bought a four-bedroom house with her sister. Their first tenant grew weed in the house for a whole year and damaged many things. They had to spend over £5,000 to repair the damages. Their second lot of tenants was a group of students who preferred to smoke weed and waste their rent money on booze and parties. She was stuck with them for a whole year. I was her third tenant. Finally, she found the kind of peace she had been looking for. I managed her house for three years. I only called her when there were major repairs, which happened just three times in three years. Meanwhile, I took care of all the minor repairs and kept her informed.

'Yes, but where do I find my landlords?' you might ask. *Everywhere.* There are millions of houses owned by millions of people. In this day and age, I cannot believe how many bank repossessions take place. There are many struggling landlords who need the help of people like you and me—we just need to reach out and find them.

I found my first landlord on the Gumtree, a free website where thousands of adverts are posted every hour. I took seven properties from that landlord alone. He had about two hundred properties in his portfolio and was struggling to fill about sixty of them. I needed him as much as he needed me. When I told him what I was doing, he said he wished he had not bought so many properties. He also said something that struck me like a crash of thunder: 'If I were in your shoes, I would do exactly what you're doing.' With his blessing, **Rent2Rent**™ makes perfect sense. We are still working together today.

In my next article, I will explore this question of tracking down landlords more thoroughly. For more details about my courses and materials to help you start your own Rent2Rent™ business, please visit my website: www.renttorent.co.uk.

Rent2Rent™: How and Where to Find Your Deals—Part 2

In my last article, I covered one of the questions people always ask me: 'Why would a landlord give me control of his or her properties?' This week, I am going to answer the second part of the question: 'Where do I find my landlords?'

I have explained that landlords can be found pretty much everywhere. My first landlord was found through my ad on the Internet. He was a struggling landlord with a large portfolio of properties. When he responded to the ad, I took seven properties from him within a matter of months.

Many people go to property networking events to find landlords with whom they can start their Rent2Rent strategy. In my honest opinion, a property networking event is the last place I would go to find a landlord because most of those landlords are also looking for ways to maximise their portfolio. In other words, they have time to implement the Rent2Rent strategy themselves.

My advice is to invest your time and effort in non-property-related networking events in your local area. Do an Internet search to find a list of all the business networking events in your area, join a few, and start your search from there. You are more likely to find solicitors, bankers, teachers, and all sorts of small business owners who have properties. You can speak with these people and grab their attention before giving their properties to letting agents. These people are property rich but time poor.

One other avenue that is more productive is a letting agent. Ninety per cent of all properties go through their hands; why not make them your ally?

I know that it can be hard and intimidating to approach agents, but when you find one, the rest tends to be easier. I remember when I first approached some letting agents; I did not know what to say or how to sell my idea to them. I was using the wrong words, which likely sounded alarm bells for them. This is part of what I teach in my workshops. My live telephone conversations with agencies are priceless tools that will give you the confidence you need to get started. With the right approach, agents will see you as an ally; they will source the right properties for you and match you with the right landlords. Do not hesitate to approach the bigger names in the letting game. After all, they have more properties, and the competition between agents is an advantage to you. The smaller agents will take your idea and implement it for themselves.

At the end of the day, Rent2Rent is a win-win solution. The landlord gets his rent guaranteed for the length of the contract, and the agents get their monthly commission during the length of the contract. The mortgage lender gets paid on time, and the tenants—especially the young ones—have a decent roof over their heads until they can afford to buy their own homes.

For more details about my courses and materials to help you start your own Rent2Rent™ business, please visit my website: www.renttorent. co.uk.

Rent2Rent™: Mortgage Defaults by Landlords

To start, I will talk briefly about the information I received through the media few weeks ago: Rent2Rent is not a good idea for landlords. I don't share the same opinion. The recession that started towards the end of 2008 has had a negative impact on tenants and landlords. Many tenants cannot afford to buy their houses or rent their flats. At the same time, many landlords struggle to fill their houses, and as a result, struggle with their mortgage payments. If landlords struggle to much, mortgage lenders may seek possession of the properties. As a Rent2Rent manager, I intervene to help the tenants get easy, comfortable, and cheap accommodations. I also help landlords prevent the loss of their houses.

Mortgage defaults by landlords, in most cases, necessitates that a landlord has a buy-to-let mortgage, which allows him or her to let the property or a residential mortgage with consent to let from the mortgagee. These two types are *authorised tenancies*. There are some rare cases of *unauthorised tenancies; this* occurs when the mortgagee is unaware that the property is let. This is a breach of contract.

As a **Rent2Rent**™ manager, if you ever find yourself in the middle of a repossession case, you should know how to negotiate the situation. You should also know your rights.

Whereas the tenancy is an authorised tenancy—that is, one for which the landlord obtained consent to let or the landlord has a buy-to-let mortgage—the mortgagee will simply take over the existing tenancy. When the tenancy is an AST, the mortgagee can act as the landlord once he or she gains possession. He or she can choose to continue to work with you or he or she can choose to serve you a section 21.

When the tenancy is an unauthorised one, you will be protected by the Mortgage Repossession Act 2010. This gives you some basic rights. The mortgagee must give you the notice of repossession hearing. The act also allows you to request a stay of possession proceedings for a period of time not exceeding two months once the mortgagee obtains a court order. In most cases, you can negotiate some grounds with the mortgagee. At the end of the day, all the other party wants is someone to pay the loan.

A couple of my students found themselves in this type of situation: the landlord did not have consent to let before letting out the property. If the property was taken through an agency, it is the agency's duty to make sure that the landlord is authorised to let. If the property is sourced directly from the landlord, it is the duty of the **Rent2Rent**™ manager to ensure that all paperwork is in place. This is why my landlord form in my legal pack is helpful and will guide you to secure the correct papers before committing yourself in a **Rent2Rent**™ deal.

For more details about my courses and materials to help you start your own Rent2Rent™ business, please visit my website: www.renttorent. co.uk.

Rent2Rent™: Option to Renew

The subject of my article this month is a specific clause called *option to renew*, which everybody implementing the **Rent2Rent**™ strategy must employ. Many landlords and letting agents may not be aware of this clause and may not have it in their standard contracts. In my view, every contract is negotiable at the beginning, so make sure you have this clause.

When you take up a property and upgrade it to the standard of your corporate tenants, you have enhanced its beauty and added value to it.

Experience taught us (i.e., me and some of my students) that when dealing with a struggling landlord who is eager to get out of his pickle as quickly as possible, it is important to instate an option to renew. If you don't, when the landlord gets out of his or her financial struggle, he or she will likely try to sell the property quickly because the property has increased in value, thanks to you. This is to your disadvantage. You can avoid this kind of situation with the correct contract.

Option to renew means that you, as a **Rent2Rent**™ agent, can request in writing (within a certain period of time) that the tenancy be renewed for an additional amount of time after the initial period has been fulfilled. You can have two or more *option to renews* and exercise your right according to the number of options you have.

Once you have that clause in writing and included in your contract, the option is entirely yours. The landlord cannot refuse if you wish to retain the property for two or three terms more. For example, if your tenancy was for an initial term of a year but included additional clauses allowing for two or three more options to renew, the landlord must keep the property for at least three years.

If you are a landlord reading this article, you might want to include an option to increase the rent with each exercise of the options. Also, you might want to stipulate that the clause ceases to exist once the number of terms have finished. Otherwise, you might end up with a perpetual option to renew.

For more details about my courses and materials to help you start your own Rent2Rent™ business, please visit my website: www.renttorent. co.uk.

Rent2Rent™: The App

How about a smartphone app that allows you to manage your **Rent2Rent™** properties on the move? You don't have to search any longer.

The **Rent2Rent™** app is available now on iPhone!

(An Android app is in the works.)

For all updates, please visit my website: www.renttorent.co.uk.

Printed in Great Britain
by Amazon